OLD MOORE'S

HOROSCOPE
AND ASTRAL
DIARY

•

ARIES

foulsham
London   New York   Toronto   Sydney

foulsham

The Publishing House, Bennetts Close,
Cippenham, Berks SL1 5AP

ISBN 0-572-02351-0

Printed in Great Britain at
Cox & Wyman Ltd, Reading

CONTENTS

OLD MOORE'S HOROSCOPE AND ASTRAL DIARY

Old Moore's Horoscope and Astral Diary represents a major departure from the usual format of publications dedicated to popular Sun-sign astrology. In this book, more attention than ever before has been focused on the discovery of the 'real you', through a wealth of astrological information, presented in an easy to follow and interesting form, and designed to provide a comprehensive insight into your fundamental nature.

The interplay of the Sun and Moon form complex cycles that are brought to bear on each of us in different ways. In the pages that follow I will explain how a knowledge of these patterns in your life can make relationships with others easier and general success more possible. Realising when your mind and body are at their most active or inactive, and at what times your greatest efforts are liable to see you winning through, can be of tremendous importance. In addition, your interaction with other zodiac types is explored, together with a comprehensive explanation of your Sun-sign nature.

In the Astral Diary you will discover a day-to-day reading covering a fifteen-month period. The readings are compiled from solar, lunar and planetary relationships as they bear upon your own zodiac sign. In addition, easy-to-follow graphic charts offer you at a glance an understanding of the way that your personal life-cycles are running; what days are best for maximum effort and when your system is likely to be regenerating.

Because some people want to look deeper into the fascinating world of personal astrology, there is a section of the book allowing a more in-depth appraisal of the all-important zodiac sign that was 'Rising' at the time of your birth. You can also look at your own personal 'Moon Sign' using simple to follow instructions to locate the position of this very significant heavenly body on the day that you were born.

From a simple-to-follow diary section, on to an intimate understanding of the ever-changing child of the solar system that you are, my Horoscope and Astral Diary will allow you to unlock potential that you never even suspected you had.

With the help and guidance of the following pages, Old Moore wishes you a happy and prosperous future.

HERE'S LOOKING AT YOU

A ZODIAC PORTRAIT OF ARIES
(21st MARCH - 20th APRIL)

The usual image of the typical Arian subject is that of the daredevil hero/heroine, champion of the underdog and conquering hero. Physically speaking, there is an Aries type, though of course there are variations within the theme. Look for fairly hurried actions, often in a slim but powerful physique. The walk is unique, with head jutting and a quick, definite gait. Aries people can be quite rash in their behaviour, so perhaps it isn't so surprising that they are more susceptible than most to cuts and bruises. Fevers and headaches are also a possibility, the more so when it is understood that the head is the part of the anatomy most influenced by this zodiac sign. The ultimate parody here is that Aries are almost certainly the most 'headstrong' of all zodiac signs.

On the rare occasions that ill health does strike, the onset is usually rapid. Fortunately the Ram has great recuperative powers and is rarely restricted by illness for any length of time. This is probably just as well, because as an Aries subject you are one of the most awkward patients possible. Unable to relax and to take the required dose of medicine, a fact which is just as true to your life generally, you always want to be on the go and do not relish either solitude or contemplation. As already mentioned, even when there is no apparent cause you are also more likely than most to fall prey to fairly severe headaches on occasion, which considering the pressure you place upon your nervous system is not particularly surprising.

THE INTENTION

The glyph for Aries shows a stylised version of the Ram's horns, which has also been understood as a representation of plant life, springing into new growth as it pushes its way through the fertile earth. This is the image of new birth, fresh beginnings, and Aries possesses a youthful spirit and great vivacity. In many ways the Ram can never grow up, though there is a wealth of difference between being child-like and childish. Here lie the positive and negative traits of Aries. When sensitive and enlightened, the Arian can be everything that is noble and honourable, though at worst we have a petulant child, jealous, brooding and vindictive. A hostile, cynical and suspicious view of life are to be avoided, in favour of open-minded optimism and a faith in the 'rightness' of creation.

What motivates Aries is the desire to seek out fresh challenges, to be creative in every sense of the word; beginnings and adventure. Retaining the creative spark that burns bright at the start of any project is not easy, but has to be learned if consistency is to be recognised and achieved. The same need for retained effort is reflected in the Arian approach to relationships. New love is exciting and utilises all the emotions as well as the libido. With time, more effort is needed to keep the relationship interesting, and this can be where the Ram falls down. Continuity is the keyword here, in every sphere of life and not merely in the practical considerations that the Ram finds so easy to deal with.

YOUR VIRTUES

If there is one particularly endearing quality common to Aries, and one that is perhaps under-valued in modern society, it is that of honesty. This is not especially evident in issues of right and wrong, more in terms of the Ram's ultimate desire to express itself, which is not possible if untruths are part of the scenario. In fact ninety-nine percent of the crazy stunts in which Aries becomes involved would not lend themselves to deceit in any case. This straight-to-the-point, no-nonsense approach to life isn't everyone's cup of tea, though if honesty truly is the best policy, then the Ram is clearly on the right track when at its best.

Aries can be very romantic, though not in the airy-fairy, dreamland sense of the word. Arians believe that they really can make all sensible dreams come true, and that means other people's as well as their own. The Ram is approachable, open, friendly and generous of heart. It is also known to be courageous, frank and possessed of reforming zeal. There is a power here that cannot be matched by any other sign. Many of the world's best rulers, historically speaking, have been born under this zodiac sign. Sad to relate, so have a fair proportion of its tyrants. There is a martial quality to the sign, so the Ram is often to be found in uniform. Of course, soldiers have to fight, something that comes naturally to the Aries subject, though that does not mean that the sign worships violence for its own sake, and though it might appear to be a contradiction in terms, the Arian can fight hard in the name of pacifism. What is implied here is absolute belief, the ability to carry things through to the bitter end, and great tenacity to work on behalf of others, once the sympathies are aroused.

YOUR VICES

One of your greatest tendencies is to become involved in things that you don't fully understand, be it a simple DIY job or running the government of a super-power. Everything is fine at the start, but it is only a matter of time before the cracks start to appear in your handiwork. Once things do go wrong, you seek to cover the cracks in order to preserve your own integrity, and this is where you can become a tyrant of the worst sort. To put it more simply, you make the start and visualise the end; what you often lack is the skill to negotiate what comes between. You often believe that the end justifies the means and need a much greater helping of method, patience and thoroughness.

Aries can often stir up trouble where none existed previously, hates authority and red-tape and can ride roughshod over the sensitivities of other people. Over-ambition and overtly aggressive behaviour are another couple of the less desirable traits, together with the gratuitous use of force on occasions in a manner that indicates an over zealous defence, even where no attack was intended. In fact, the ego here is really quite frail, which can make you even more dominant as a compensation.

LIVING A HAPPY LIFE

The problem with Aries seems to be in finding the right balance to suit your combative Martian nature, at the same time cultivating a degree of sensitivity that allows your various skills to be put to the best possible use.

There is little doubt that in terms of career, you need to be at the forefront, in a managerial position or at the very least in charge of your own work. You enjoy the cut and thrust of trouble-shooting, but hate to be tied down by convention or red-tape. Many Arians choose self-employment as a logical step and can often be very happy managing their own lot in life. You would soon become very unhappy if you were tied to any job that meant constantly having to bow and scrape to others, so the service industries are probably not for you. Amongst the caring professions that the sign is inclined to follow, the vocation of surgeon comes high up the list of possibilities. Your Martian temperament, as is the case with your astrological cousin Scorpio, means that you are happy to swap the more natural sword for a life-saving scalpel.

When you are not at work, the sporting world could captivate your attention and can also supply you with the all-important competitive edge, so crucial to the well-being of your unique and assertive nature. Physical contact sports most probably appeal the most, though be careful that your desire to win does not become more important than the simple act of taking part. In this, as in so much else, you are inclined to try too hard for your own good and may destroy the whole point of the exercise all too easily.

Keeping well is so often a matter of being physically fit and personally happy as far as you are concerned. Watch out for those tell-tale headaches, a warning of nervous exhaustion, and do make certain that you get enough rest. Eat a balanced diet if you can, and don't wolf down your food like a maniac. There are very few vegetarians amongst the ranks of your sign, though an accumulation of stress, too much work, together with a diet that is rich in fat, can all contribute to eventual ill-health, so some concession to healthy living may not be a bad thing.

In relationships, look for a partner who can deal with your tremendous energy, but who can also encourage you to utilise your own latent sensitivity. Long-term commitment is important, and the establishment of a lasting relationship, where friendship and shared interests can make up for any shortfall once things cool down a little physically.

WHAT'S RISING

YOUR RISING SIGN AND PERSONALITY

Perhaps you have come across this term 'Rising Sign' when looking at other books on astrology and may have been somewhat puzzled as to what it actually means. To those not accustomed to astrological jargon it could sound somewhat technical and mysterious, though in fact, in terms of your own personal birth chart, it couldn't be simpler. The Rising Sign is simply that part of the zodiac occupying the eastern horizon at the time of your birth. Because it is a little more difficult to discover than your sun-sign, many writers of popular astrology have tended to ignore it, which is a great shame, because, together with the Sun, your Rising Sign is the single most important factor in terms of setting your personality. So much so, that no appraisal of your astrological nature could be complete without it.

Your Rising Sign, also known as your 'Ascendant' or 'Ascending Sign' plays a great part in your looks - yes, astrology can even predict what you are going to be like physically. In fact, this is a very interesting point, because there appears to be a tie- in between astrology and genetics. Professional Astrologers for centuries have noted the close relationship that often exists between the astrological birth chart of parents and those of their offspring, so that, if you look like your Mother or Father, chances are that there is a close astrological tie-up. Rising signs especially appear to be handed down through families.

The first impression that you get, in an astrological sense, upon meeting a stranger, is not related to their sun-sign but to the zodiac sign that was rising at the moment they came into the world. The Rising Sign is particularly important because it modifies the way that you display your Sun-sign to the world at large. A good example of this might be that of Britain's best- known ex- Prime minister, Margaret Thatcher. This dynamic and powerful lady is a Libran by Sun-sign placing, indicating a light-hearted nature, pleasure loving and very flexible. However, Mrs Thatcher has Scorpio as her Rising Sign, bringing a steely determination and a tremendous capacity for work. It also bestows an iron will and the power to thrive under pressure.

WHAT'S RISING?

Here lies the true importance of the Rising Sign, for Mr Thatcher almost certainly knows a woman who most other people do not. The Rising Sign is a protective shell, and not until we know someone quite well do we start to discover the Sun-sign nature that hides within this often tough outer coat of astrological making. Your Rising Sign also represents your basic self-image, the social mask that is often so useful; and even if you don't think that you conform to the interpretation of your Ascendant, chances are that other people will think that you do.

The way that an individual looks, walks, sits and generally presents themselves to the world is all down to the Rising Sign. For example, a person possessed of Gemini Rising is apt to be very quick, energetic in all movements, deliberate in mannerisms and with a cheerful disposition. A bearer of a Taurean Ascendant on the other hand would probably not be so tall, more solid generally, quieter in aspect and calmer in movement. Once you come to understand the basics of astrology it is really very easy to pick out the Rising Signs of people that you come across, even though the Sun-sign is often more difficult to pin down. Keep an eye open for the dynamic and positive Aries Rising individual, or the retiring, shy but absolutely magnetic quality of of the Piscean Ascendant. Of course, in astrology, nothing is quite that simple. The position of a vast array of heavenly bodies at the time of birth also has to be taken into account, particularly that of the Moon and the inner planets Mercury and Venus. Nevertheless a knowledge of your Rising sign can be an invaluable aid in getting to know what really makes you tick as an individual.

To ascertain the exact degree of your Rising sign takes a little experience and recourse to some special material. However, I have evolved a series of tables that will enable you to discover at a glance what your Rising Sign is likely to be. All you need to know is the approximate time of your birth. At the back of the book you will find the necessary table related to your Sun-sign. Simply look down the left-hand column until you find your approximate time of birth, am or pm. Now scan across the top of the table to the place where your date of birth is shown. Look for the square where the two pieces of information connect and there is your Rising Sign. Now that you know what your Rising Sign is, read on, and learn even more about the fascinating interplay of astrological relationship.

ARIES WITH ARIES RISING

As with all people who share the same Rising sign and Sun sign, you would be considered by the world at large to be very typical of your part of the zodiac. This also infers that you are what you appear to be, with few frills and fancies to confuse the people that you come across as to your real motivations and intentions. You are cheerful in attitude, sometimes a little too brusque for your own good, but basically kind hearted and willing to help others. Not everyone will take to you as an individual, though you do have both the power and determination to make a great success of your life. Confidence is some-thing that others assume you have in abundance, though in reality your ego is more fragile than you would be willing to let on. You may lack tact, but not kindness, and can be relied upon to offer protection and help to those people who you choose to take under your wing.

ARIES WITH TAURUS RISING

As far as the text book Aries subject is concerned, you are not at all typical. For a start, you are inclined to bottle up your feelings, instead of ranting and raving from time to time, as the more typical Ram is inclined to do. In a way this can be a problem because you are more susceptible to nervous tension than many of your astrological cousins, simply because you cannot let go.

There are aspects of your Aries self that you don't really care for and as a result you cultivate the more cultured and refined aspects more common under the rulership of the Bull. You do have the ability to channel your ambitions into practical areas and can be very successful professionally. Your basic desire is to build permanent structures into your life, whether in your job, home or relationship. Thought and care come easily to you, though some better outlets for tension would help since both the Ram and the Bull can be quite nervy in their own very different ways. Comfort and security appeal to you through the sign of Taurus, even though Aries is less concerned about such matters. You are an admirable friend and colleague, and all the more so when the nature of the individuals with whom you are associated meshes well with your own. On the other hand you could make a formidable enemy.

ARIES WITH GEMINI RISING

Here we find a fairly typical Arian, with the usual qualities of extroversion, restlessness and a quick-witted self-assurance. You chat on like a radio, though most of what you have to say is of great interest to a broad cross-section of the many people that you come across. Conversation is an important factor, you don't care for silences and will search around for any suitable listener. Aries with Gemini Rising folk are not beyond listening to gossip, or manufacturing it for that matter. Despite your penchant for hearsay however, one of your most redeeming features is the light touch that you have in your dealings with other individuals. A humorous and engaging nature assures you of popularity with a thousand and one acquaintances. Although you are not as forthright or direct as the really typical Ram, the greater tolerance you possess can be a valuable asset. In social encounters the more Mercurial qualities of Gemini would be more likely to predominate. All the same, the strength of the Ram is available when it is needed most.

ARIES WITH CANCER RISING

Your tendency to adopt an 'I know what's best for you' attitude can be very annoying to other people, though it is what one might expect when two such different signs as these come together. You really do believe that you have the key to everyone's well-being, even when you can be accused of being something of a bully on account of the methods that you use. You do have a very strong intuition that can be used successfully on your way up to the top, for the desire to succeed is just as strong with Cancer Rising as with almost any other companion sign. There is a difference here though, because the desire you have to come good is genuinely geared towards offering your partner and family the material comfort that is so important to you. You don't really like to wait for anything and so impatience is something that you have to deal with in a positive manner.

Despite your ultimate ability to succeed in life, you may lack confidence, particularly in an emotional sense. In a relationship you must feel secure, even though you often pretend that this is not the case. This need can make you 'cling' much more than would be the case for Aries alone.

ARIES WITH LEO RISING

Combined with another Fire sign, such as Aries, the proud Lion goes from strength to strength here. There is a great need for ego boosting on a daily basis and a strong desire for the individual with this combination to get his or her own way. Still, you possess a big heart and a genuine desire to help other people if you can. Whatever you do on account of others is done with no strings attached and your generosity in everything should be legendary. Strangely enough, receiving is something you are not quite so good at, possibly because you prefer to have others in your debt than you do to be in theirs. Travel is something that you take on board readily, preferably to foreign parts, and you can be restless in the mental sphere too. Interesting and off-beat subjects can be guaranteed to hold your attention more than routine and tedious matters, which, with all that fire on board soon leave you cold. You need a flexible and interesting life, with plenty of scope for individuality.

ARIES WITH VIRGO RISING

An unusual combination this one; the rather restless Fire of Aries and the steady Earth restraint of Virgo, making for a distinctly complex personality. Beneath the quieter Virgo outer shell is a lively individual, not exactly bursting to get out, though certainly around at times of excitement, or when the personality is subjected to stimulants such as alcohol. You like a friendly chat, even if in a low-key way you tend to be somewhat bossy. There is little that can be done to find an ultimate winner in the internal struggle between selfishness and selflessness that constantly runs its course within you and, in the main, others see the caring side in any case.

It sometimes looks as if you took a degree in humility and yet you fare very well in big business; patient enough to wait until the time is right and then striking like lightening. The greatest surprise to a disbelieving world is that you invariably get your own way, because few people would notice your ability to manipulate situations and people. In the main this is an ability that is utilised on behalf of others, though it would make you a formidable enemy if you considered yourself to be seriously crossed. People who do know you well would never seek to force you into a corner.

ARIES WITH LIBRA RISING

Libra does bring a gentler aspect to bear on the generally volatile Aries component of your nature and makes for a far more complex character than would be expected from Aries alone. All the same, you can be fairly short-tempered and will not suffer fools gladly. You are quite prepared to take the initiative in social encounters, when beginning new projects or laying down plans generally. On occasions you manage to score your points by being unobtrusive, so there can be a few contradictions thrown up by this combination. Perhaps your best talent lies in your ability to make others feel that they are very important, which means that they will do almost anything for you in return. This makes you socially popular and assures you of avid support. Unlike Aries, you have as much interest in the world at large as you do with regard to your own ideas and efforts.

In your own circle you will be considered to be something of a 'character', you can think long and hard before deciding on important matters. However, once you have made up your mind you can strike like a cobra.

ARIES WITH SCORPIO RISING

Secrecy is your main component, playing all your cards of emotional considerations and even practical intentions close to your chest. This means that only the selective few ever learn what really makes you tick as an individual, and in the main you are happy to keep things this way. There is little doubt that you are intensely psychic, which is why you quickly learn to listen to your deepest feelings and react according to them. Strangely enough, for a person who is capable of being so sensitive, you do have the ability to be quite calculating, and even cruel on occasions. The saving grace is that you are always full of apologies when you know that you have hurt another, and you can do a tremendous amount for the hungry, wretched and dispossessed of the world. You can be very practical and a workaholic, though your family is very important, likewise the cultivation of one or two very close friends. Some caution is necessary though because a number of well-meaning but despotic individuals in the past have shared this combination with you. On the other hand, so have some saints.

ARIES WITH SAGITTARIUS RISING

This combination of Fire signs makes for the sort of individual who is possessed of a child-like naivety on occasions, underpinning a nature that is really quite astute and a determination that is second to none. Getting to grips with the everyday concerns of life isn't always too easy for you, though you are generally forgiven for the fact because your nature is so easy-going and you have a disarming honesty to match any in the zodiac. It is true that you can be a little accident-prone, and that not all your schemes turn out as you might intend, despite the fact that you have an idealised view of the world and never stop seeking the sort of heaven-on-earth which somehow always remains just a little out of reach. Despite your warm-hearted candour and tendency to hurt others without realising, you are daring, adventurous, and too brave for your own good on occasions since you can get yourself into the most awkward situations as a result. Perhaps just a little more caution would be a good thing generally, together with a less impetuous approach especially to relationships.

ARIES WITH CAPRICORN RISING

Since Aries and Capricorn are quite antagonistic to each other, as far as personal qualities are concerned, it is up to you to try and balance these conflicting elements in your overall personality. You have impatience and immediacy, courtesy of the Ram, but also the cautious, reticent nature of the Goat. This creates a stop-start effect and can mean quite a wait in order to reach your appointed destination. Others would see you as being taciturn, and a little too reserved for an Aries, partly because you suffer from a basic doubt about your own abilities to make it in the world. Instinctively it occurs that somewhere inside you is a winner, a champion and a gigantic success. The trouble is that this quality isn't always so easy to find. At your strongest, you have a powerful presence and a comic sense of humour. On top of this you have stubborn, but intelligent opinions even though you may often be reserved in public. Such contradicting qualities could make it difficult for other people to get to know you quickly, though friends, once made, last for life. In business you could go far because you have all the necessary gifts to reach the top, and stay there.

ARIES WITH AQUARIUS RISING

The Ram with Aquarius rising reverts to type in certain ways. For instance you are not adverse to speaking your mind when it comes to taking a particular stance on any issue. In fact you are usually out there on your soapbox making sure that your points of view are being given due consideration. You are capable of beginning arguments, apparently merely for the sake of doing so, yet from your own side of the fence it always appears that you have something vitally important to say. Unfortunately, others may not always feel quite the same. It is important that you allow others to express their opinions too and that your debates do not take on the appearance of a monologue. In general you recognise that you live to learn. Education is likely to be one of the main concerns in your life and you readily assume the role of lecturer in order to pass information to others. Energy can be channelled into writing, travelling or spending long hours on the phone to your intellectual friends. You possess a speed of thought that others would find unbelievable and your quick and ready wit will attract many friends.

ARIES WITH PISCES RISING

The poor Aries with Pisces Rising often finds it difficult to come to terms in a conscious sense with the qualities usually attributed to the Ram. Much of that fearless spirit has been demoted to the level of fantasy behind the dreamy Piscean Rising sign. This inability to look the world directly in the eye may be problematic for those of you with this combination. If so, what you need to do is confront yourself as honestly as possible and get in touch with the inner-self which is your birthright. The sensitivity and compassion of your Rising sign are gifts which can be put to use effectively, yet the more negative traits of a strong Piscean influence can cause more than their fair share of emotional chaos. Deep within is the fearless bold Ram and when you can overcome your retiring nature in social situations, others find your poetic style quite appealing. You do have some surprises up your sleeve, when others get to know you well, and your paradoxical nature is a puzzle that is inspirational to almost everyone you meet. You should make a fine business person.

ARIES
IN LOVE AND FRIENDSHIP

WANT TO KNOW HOW WELL YOU GET ON WITH OTHER ZODIAC SIGNS?

THE TABLES BELOW DEAL WITH LOVE AND FRIENDSHIP

THE MORE HEARTS THERE ARE AGAINST ANY SIGN OF THE ZODIAC, THE BETTER THE CHANCE OF CUPID'S DART SCORING A DIRECT HIT.

THE SMILES OF FRIENDSHIP DISPLAY HOW WELL YOU WORK OR ASSOCIATE WITH ALL THE OTHER SIGNS OF THE ZODIAC.

Love (hearts)					Sign	Friendship (smiles)				
♥	♥	♥	♥	♥	**ARIES**	☺	☺	☺	☺	
	♥	♥	♥	♥	**TAURUS**	☺	☺	☺		
		♥	♥	♥	**GEMINI**	☺	☺	☺	☺	
		♥	♥	♥	**CANCER**	☺	☺	☺		
♥	♥	♥	♥	♥	**LEO**	☺	☺	☺	☺	☺
	♥	♥	♥	♥	**VIRGO**	☺	☺	☺		
			♥	♥	**LIBRA**	☺	☺			
		♥	♥	♥	**SCORPIO**	☺	☺	☺	☺	
♥	♥	♥	♥	♥	**SAGITTARIUS**	☺	☺	☺	☺	☺
		♥	♥	♥	**CAPRICORN**	☺	☺	☺	☺	
		♥	♥	♥	**AQUARIUS**	☺	☺	☺		
			♥	♥	**PISCES**	☺	☺			

THE MOON AND THE PART IT PLAYS IN YOUR LIFE

In astrology the Moon is probably the single most important heavenly body after the Sun. It's unique position, as partner to the Earth on its journey around the solar system means that the Moon appears to pass through the signs of the zodiac extremely quickly. The zodiac position of the Moon at the time of your birth plays a great part in personal character and is especially significant in the build-up of your emotional nature.

SUN MOON CYCLES

The first lunar cycle deals with the part the position of the Moon plays relative to your Sun sign. I have made the fluctuations of this pattern easy for you to understand by means of a simple cyclic graph. It appears on the first page of each 'Your Month At A Glance', under the title 'Highs and Lows'. The graph displays the lunar cycle and you will soon learn to understand how its movements have a bearing on your level of energy and your abilities.

YOUR OWN MOON SIGN

Discovering the position of the Moon at the time of your birth has always been notoriously difficult because tracking the complex zodiac positions of the Moon is not easy. This process has been reduced to three simple stages with Old Moore's unique Lunar Tables. A breakdown of the Moon's zodiac positions can be found from page 24 onwards, so that once you know what your Moon sign is, you can see what part this plays in the overall build-up of your personal character.

If you follow the instructions on the next page you will soon be able to work out exactly what zodiac sign the Moon occupied on the day that you were born and you can then go on to compare the reading for this position with those of your Sun sign and your Ascendant. It is partly the comparison between these three important positions that goes towards making you the unique individual you truly are.

HOW TO DISCOVER YOUR MOON SIGN

This is a three stage process. You may need a pen and a piece of paper but if you follow the instructions below the process should only take a minute or two.

STAGE 1 First of all you need to know the Moon Age at the time of your birth. If you look at Moon Table 1, on page 21, you will find all the years between 1905 and 1996 down the left side. Find the year of your birth and then trace across to the right to the month of your birth. Where the two intersect you will find a number. This is the date of the New Moon in the month that you were born. You now need to count forward the number of days between the New Moon and your own birthday. For example, if the New Moon in the month of your birth was shown as being the 6th and you were born on the 20th, your Moon Age Day would be 14. If the New Moon in the month of your birth came after your birthday, you need to count forward from the New Moon in the previous month. Whatever the result, jot this number down so that you do not forget it.

STAGE 2 Take a look at Moon Table 2 on page 22. Down the left hand column look for the date of your birth. Now trace across to the month of your birth. Where the two meet you will find a letter. Copy this letter down alongside your Moon Age Day.

STAGE 3 Moon Table 3 on page 22 will supply you with the zodiac sign the Moon occupied on the day of your birth. Look for your Moon Age Day down the left hand column and then for the letter you found in Stage 2. Where the two converge you will find a zodiac sign and this is the sign occupied by the Moon on the day that you were born.

YOUR ZODIAC MOON SIGN EXPLAINED

You will find a profile of all zodiac Moon Signs on pages 24 to 29, showing in yet another way how astrology helps to make you into the individual that you are. In each daily entry of the Astral Diary you can find the zodiac position of the Moon for every day of the year. This allows you to also discover your lunar birthdays. Since the Moon passes through all the signs of the zodiac in about a month, you can expect something like twelve lunar birthdays each year. At these times you are likely to be emotionally steady and able to make the sort of decisions that have real, lasting value.

NEW MOON TABLE 1

YEAR	FEB	MAR	APR	YEAR	FEB	MAR	APR
1905	5	5	4	1950	16	18	17
1906	23	24	23	1951	6	7	6
1907	12	14	12	1952	25	25	24
1908	2	3	2	1953	14	15	13
1909	20	21	20	1954	3	5	3
1910	9	11	9	1955	22	24	22
1911	28	30	28	1956	11	12	11
1912	17	19	18	1957	–	1/31	29
1913	6	7	6	1958	18	20	19
1914	24	26	24	1959	7	9	8
1915	14	15	13	1960	26	27	26
1916	3	5	3	1961	15	16	15
1917	22	23	22	1962	5	6	5
1918	11	12	11	1963	23	25	23
1919	–	2/31	30	1964	13	14	12
1920	19	20	18	1965	1	2	1
1921	8	9	8	1966	19	21	20
1922	26	28	27	1967	9	10	9
1923	15	17	16	1968	28	29	28
1924	5	5	4	1969	17	18	16
1925	23	24	23	1970	6	7	6
1926	12	14	12	1971	25	26	25
1927	2	3	2	1972	14	15	13
1928	19	21	20	1973	4	5	3
1929	9	11	9	1974	22	24	22
1930	28	30	28	1975	11	12	11
1931	17	19	18	1976	29	30	29
1932	6	7	6	1977	18	19	18
1933	24	26	24	1978	7	9	7
1934	14	15	13	1979	26	27	26
1935	3	5	3	1980	15	16	15
1936	22	23	21	1981	4	6	4
1937	11	12	12	1982	23	24	23
1938	–	2/31	30	1983	13	14	13
1939	19	20	19	1984	1	2	1
1940	8	9	7	1985	19	21	20
1941	26	27	26	1986	9	10	9
1942	15	16	15	1987	28	29	28
1943	4	6	4	1988	17	18	16
1944	24	24	22	1989	6	7	6
1945	12	14	12	1990	25	26	25
1946	2	3	2	1991	14	15	13
1947	19	21	20	1992	3	4	3
1948	9	11	9	1993	22	24	22
1949	27	29	28	1994	10	12	11

MOON TABLE 2		
DAY	MAR	APR
1	F	J
2	G	J
3	G	J
4	G	J
5	G	J
6	G	J
7	G	J
8	G	J
9	G	J
10	G	J
11	G	K
12	H	K
13	H	K
14	H	K
15	H	K
16	H	K
17	H	K
18	H	K
19	H	K
20	H	K
21	H	L
22	I	L
23	I	L
24	I	L
25	I	L
26	I	L
27	I	L
28	I	L
29	I	L
30	I	L
31	I	–

MOON TABLE 3						
M/D	F	G	H	I	J	K	L
0	PI	PI	AR	AR	AR	TA	TA
1	PI	AR	AR	AR	TA	TA	TA
2	AR	AR	AR	TA	TA	TA	GE
3	AR	AR	TA	TA	TA	GE	GE
4	AR	TA	TA	GE	GE	GE	GE
5	TA	TA	GE	GE	GE	CA	CA
6	TA	GE	GE	GE	CA	CA	CA
7	GE	GE	GE	CA	CA	CA	LE
8	GE	GE	CA	CA	CA	LE	LE
9	CA	CA	CA	CA	LE	LE	VI
10	CA	CA	LE	LE	LE	VI	VI
11	CA	LE	LE	LE	VI	VI	VI
12	LE	LE	LE	VI	VI	VI	LI
13	LE	LE	VI	VI	VI	LI	LI
14	VI	VI	VI	LI	LI	LI	LI
15	VI	VI	LI	LI	LI	SC	SC
16	VI	LI	LI	LI	SC	SC	SC
17	LI	LI	LI	SC	SC	SC	SA
18	LI	LI	SC	SC	SC	SA	SA
19	LI	SC	SC	SC	SA	SA	SA
20	SC	SC	SA	SA	SA	CP	CP
21	SC	SA	SA	SA	CP	CP	CP
22	SC	SA	SA	CP	CP	CP	AQ
23	SA	SA	CP	CP	CP	AQ	AQ
24	SA	CP	CP	CP	AQ	AQ	AQ
25	CP	CP	AQ	AQ	AQ	PI	PI
26	CP	AQ	AQ	AQ	PI	PI	PI
27	AQ	AQ	AQ	PI	PI	PI	AR
28	AQ	AQ	PI	PI	PI	AR	AR
29	AQ	PI	PI	PI	AR	AR	AR

AR = ARIES   TA = TAURUS   GE = GEMINI
CA = CANCER   LE = LEO   VI = VIRGO   LI = LIBRA
SC = SCORPIO   SA = SAGITTARIUS   CP = CAPRICORN
AQ = AQUARIUS   PI = PISCES

RETROGRADE MERCURY

Before we see how the various zodiac positions of the Moon can have a bearing on you in a day to day sense, we need to look at another particularly important factor in your life, namely Retrograde Mercury.

A retrograde planet is one that appears, when viewed from the Earth, to be moving backwards through space. Of course this state of affairs is quite impossible, since planetary orbits around the Sun maintain only one direction. The reason that planets sometimes appear to be travelling backwards is due to the unique orbital position of the Earth within the solar system. When a planet seems to be running retrograde it is merely a line of sight effect caused by the relative positions of the planets at any given point in time. All of the planets, with the exception of the Moon, which is a satellite of the Earth and not strictly speaking a planet in its own right, can run retrograde. In the case of the larger planets, from Jupiter outwards, the retrograde periods can sometimes last many weeks.

Astrologers have always been fascinated by retrograde planetary movement and pay great attention to it, especially when constructing personal birth charts. However, in our lightening fast lives, no retrograde position is more important than that of tiny Mercury, which orbits closer to the Sun than any other planet in the solar system.

Mercury is the natural ruler of communication and one of the most obvious effects of its retrograde movement is that most forms of human interaction can suffer a little as a result. This can have a bearing on all human beings and it is amazing how often international negotiations, treaties and the like undergo setbacks if undertaken whilst Mercury is retrograde. In a more personal sense you will need to be aware on such days that it will be harder to get your message across to others. Greater tact and diplomacy are recommended and some patience in your general dealings with the world at large.

A further word of warning relates to mechanical objects, especially those such as computers, which also deal with communication. If you experience a difficulty in this direction, it will almost certainly occur whilst Mercury is retrograde. Such trends are seldom severe, but where you see the symbol ♦, immediately prior to the Moon Age Day on any Astral Diary entry, some slight precautions would be no bad thing.

MOON SIGNS

MOON IN ARIES

You have a strong imagination and a desire to do things in your own way. Showing no lack of courage you can forge your own path through life with great determination.

Originality is one of your most important attributes, you are seldom stuck for an idea though your mind is very changeable and more attention might be given over to one job at once. Few have the ability to order you around and you can be quite quick tempered. A calm and relaxed attitude is difficult for you to adopt but because you put tremendous pressure on your nervous system it is vitally important for you to forget about the cut and thrust of life from time to time. It would be fair to say that you rarely get the rest that you both need and deserve and because of this there is a chance that your health could break down from time to time.

Emotionally speaking you can be a bit of a mess if you don't talk to the folks that you are closest to and work out how you really feel about things. Once you discover that there are people willing to help you there is suddenly less necessity for trying to tackle everything yourself.

MOON IN TAURUS ✓ ＩＡＮ

The Moon in Taurus at the time you were born gives you a courteous and friendly manner that is likely to assure you of many friends.

The good things in life mean a great deal to you for Taurus is an Earth sign and delights in experiences that please the senses. This probably makes you a lover of good food and drink and might also mean that you have to spend time on the bathroom scales balancing the delight of a healthy appetite with that of looking good which is equally important to you.

Emotionally you are fairly stable and once you have opted for a set of standards you are inclined to stick to them because Taurus is a Fixed sign and doesn't respond particularly well to change. Intuition also plays an important part in your life.

MOON IN GEMINI

The Moon in the sign of Gemini gives a warm-hearted character, full of sympathy and usually ready to help those in difficulty. In some matters you are very reserved, whilst at other times you are articulate and chatty: this is part of the paradox of Gemini which always brings duplicity to the nature. The knowledge you possess of local and national affairs is very good, this strengthens and enlivens your intellect making you good company and endowing you with many friends. Most of the people with whom you mix have a high opinion of you and will stand ready to leap to your defence, not that this is generally necessary for although you are not martial by nature, you are more than capable of defending yourself verbally.

Travel plays an important part in your life and the naturally inquisitive quality of your mind allows you to benefit greatly from changes in scenery. The more you mix with people from different cultures and backgrounds the greater your interest in life becomes and intellectual stimulus is the meat and drink of the Gemini individual.

You can gain through reading and writing as well as the cultivation of artistic pursuits but you do need plenty of rest in order to avoid fatigue.

MOON IN CANCER

Moon in Cancer at the time of birth is a most fortunate position since the sign of Cancer is the Moon's natural home. This means that the qualities of compassion and understanding given by the Moon are especially enhanced in your nature and you cope quite well with emotional pressures that would bother others. You are friendly and sociably inclined. Domestic tasks don't really bother you and your greatest love is likely to be for home and family. Your surroundings are particularly important and you hate squalor and filth.

Your basic character, although at times changeable like the Moon itself, depends upon symmetry. Little wonder then that you are almost certain to have a love of music and poetry. Not surprising either that you do all within your power to make your surroundings comfortable and harmonious, not only for yourself, but on behalf of the folk who mean so much to you.

MOON IN LEO

You are especially ambitious and self-confident. The best qualities of both the Moon and the Sign of Leo come together here to ensure that you are warm-hearted and fair, characteristics that are almost certain to show through no matter what other planetary positions your chart contains.

You certainly don't lack the ability to organise, either yourself or those around you, and you invariably rise to a position of responsibility no matter what you decide to do with your life. Perhaps it is just as well because you don't enjoy being an 'also ran' and would much rather be an important part of a small organisation than a menial in a larger one.

In love you are likely to be lucky and happy provided that you put in that extra bit of effort and you can be relied upon to build comfortable home surroundings for yourself and also those for whom you feel a particular responsibility. It is likely that you will have a love of pleasure and sport and perhaps a fondness for music and literature. Life brings you many rewards, though most of them are as a direct result of the effort that you are able to put in on your own behalf. All the same you are inclined to be more lucky than average and will usually make the best of any given circumstance.

MOON IN VIRGO

This position of the Moon endows you with good mental abilities and a keen receptive memory. By nature you are probably quite reserved, nevertheless you have many friends, especially of the opposite sex, and you gain a great deal as a result of these associations. Marital relationships need to be discussed carefully and kept as harmonious as possible because personal attachments can be something of a problem to you if sufficient attention is not given to the way you handle them.

You are not ostentatious or pretentious, two characteristics that are sure to improve your popularity. Talented and persevering you possess artistic qualities and are a good home-maker. Earning your honours through genuine merit you can work long and hard towards your objectives but probably show very little pride in your genuine achievements. Many short journeys will be undertaken in your life.

MOON IN LIBRA

With the Moon in Libra you have a popular nature and don't find it particularly difficult to make friends. Most folk like you, probably more than you think, and all get together's would be more fun with you present. Libra, for all its good points, is not the most stable of Astrological signs and as a result your emotions can prove to be a little unstable too. Although the Moon in Libra is generally said to be good for love and marriage, the position of the Sun, and also the Rising Sign, in your own birth chart will have a greater than usual effect on your emotional and loving qualities.

You cannot live your life in isolation and must rely on other people, who are likely to play an important part in your decision making. Co-operation is crucial for you because Libra represents the 'balance' of life that can only be achieved through harmonious relationships. An offshoot of this fact is that you do not enjoy being disliked and, like all Librans are a natural diplomat.

Conformity is not always easy for you, because Libra is an Air sign and likes to go its own way.

MOON IN SCORPIO

Some people might call you a little pushy, in fact all you really want to do is live your life to the full, and to protect yourself and your family from the pressures of life that you recognise all too readily. You should avoid giving the impression of being sarcastic or too impulsive, at the same time using your energies wisely and in a constructive manner.

Nobody could doubt your courage which is great, and you invariably achieve what you set out to do, by force of personality as well as by the effort that you are able to put in. You are fond of mystery and are probably quite perceptive as to the outcome of situations and events.

Problems can arise in your relationships with members of the opposite sex, so before you commit yourself emotionally it is very important to examine your motives carefully and ensure that the little demon, jealousy, always a problem with Scorpio positions, does not cloud your judgement in love matches. You need to travel and can make gains as a result.

MOON IN SAGITTARIUS

The Moon in Sagittarius helps to make you a generous individual with humanitarian qualities and a kind heart. Restlessness may be an endemic part of your character for your mind is seldom still. Perhaps because of this you have an overwhelming need for change that could lead you to several major moves during your adult life. You are probably a reasonably sporting sort of person and not afraid to stand your ground on the occasions when you know that you are correct in your judgement. What you have to say goes right to the heart of the matter and your intuition is very good.

At work you are quick and efficient in whatever you choose to do, and because you are versatile you make an ideal employee. Ideally you need work that is intellectually demanding because you are no drudge and would not enjoy tedious routines. In relationships you anger quickly if faced with stupidity or deception, though you are just as quick to forgive and forget. Emotionally there are times when you allow your heart rule your head.

MOON IN CAPRICORN

Born with the Moon in Capricorn, you are popular and may come into the public eye in one way or another. Your administrative ability is good and you are a capable worker. The watery Moon is not entirely at home in the Earth sign of Capricorn and as a result difficulties can be experienced, especially in the early years of life. Some initial lack of creative ability and indecision has to be overcome before the true qualities of patience and perseverance inherent in Capricorn can show through.

If caution is exercised in financial affairs you can accumulate wealth with the passing of time but you will always have to be careful about forming any partnerships because you are open to deception more than most. Under such circumstances you would be well advised to gain professional advice before committing yourself. Many people with the Moon in Capricorn take a healthy interest in social or welfare work. The organisational skills that you have, together with a genuine sympathy for others, means that you are ideally suited to this kind of career or pastime.

MOON IN AQUARIUS

With the Moon in Aquarius you are an active and agreeable person with a friendly easy going sort of nature. Being sympathetic to the needs of other people you flourish best in an easy going atmosphere. You are broad minded, just, and open to suggestion, though as with all faces of Aquarius the Moon here brings an unconventional quality that not everyone would find easy to understand.

You have a liking for anything strange and curious as well a fascination for old articles and places. Journeys to such locations would suit you doubly because you love to travel and can gain a great deal from the trips that you make. Political, scientific and educational work might all be of interest to you and you would gain from a career in some new and exciting branch of science or technology.

Money-wise, you make gains through innovation as much as by concentration and it isn't unusual to find Lunar Aquarians tackling more than one job at the same time. In love you are honest and kind.

MOON IN PISCES

This position assures you of a kind sympathetic nature, somewhat retiring at times but always taking account of others and doing your best to help them. As with all planets in Pisces there is bound to be some misfortunes on the way through life. In particular, relationships of a personal nature can be problematic and often through no real fault of your own. Inevitably though, suffering brings a better understanding, both of yourself and of the world around you. With a fondness for travel you appreciate beauty and harmony wherever you encounter them and hate disorder and strife.

You are probably very fond of literature and could make a good writer or speaker yourself. The imagination that you possess can be readily translated into creativity and you might come across as an incurable romantic. Being naturally receptive your intuition is strong, in many cases verging on a mediumistic quality that sets you apart from the world. You might not be rich in hard cash terms and yet the gifts that you possess and display, when used properly, are worth more than gold.

MORE ABOUT THE MOON

In addition to your lunar birthdays, you can also gain a better understanding of the way cycles work in your life by keeping track of the Moon
Age Day. You probably already know your Moon Age Day because it was
the first stage of the process to establish your Moon's zodiac sign. If you
have any doubts, look back to pages 19 and 20.

Keeping track of Moon Age Days can be very useful because you are
likely to be at the peak of your personal life cycles at those times when
the Moon reaches the same Moon Age Day each month as the one it had
achieved at the time of your birth. So, for example, if you were born on
Moon Age Day 12, you will find that around the same Moon Age Day each
month your decision making skills are honed to perfection and that you
find yourself in a position to take almost any bull by the horns. You can
find the Moon Age Day to the right of the date on each daily entry in the
Astral Diary.

THE MOON AGE QUICK REFERENCE TABLE

The situation goes much further however because all facets of astrology
respond to 'resonances'. Certain Moon Age Days have much in common
with your own, which makes those days more significant to you. Conversely,
there are going to be Moon Age Days that are not so positive in relation
to your own. To make the situation easier to understand you can look at
the table on the page opposite. Scanning down the left hand column you
can find your own Moon Age Day. How your own Moon Age Day relates
to all the others can be seen by tracing along to the right.

+ Days harmonious with your own Moon Age Day and so find you more
positive, anxious to make the most of every opportunity and keen to get
ahead.

- Days are likely to be less favourable and represent days when it would
not be sensible to take any unnecessary chances. You could feel just a
little out of sorts and might be best avoiding too much exertion.

* Days occur only once each lunar month. Such times could well find you
feeling on top form and very anxious to pitch yourself into any situation
with absolute confidence. If you act with determination on * days, your
chances of ultimate success could be that much higher.

MOON AGE QUICK REFERENCE TABLE

SIGNIFICANT MOON AGE DAYS

		+ Days	- Days	* Days
Y	0	4, 6, 12, 14, 19, 21, 25, 28	9, 16, 23	0
	1	5, 7, 13, 15, 20, 22, 26, 29	10, 17, 24	1
	2	0, 6, 8, 14, 16, 21, 23, 27	11, 18, 25	2
O	3	1, 7, 9, 15, 17, 22, 24, 28	12, 19, 26	3
U	4	2, 8, 10, 16, 18, 23, 25, 29	13, 20, 27	4
R	5	0, 3, 4, 9, 11, 17, 19, 24, 26	14, 21, 28	5
	6	1, 4, 5, 10, 12, 18, 20, 25, 27	5, 22, 29	6
	7	2, 5, 11, 13, 19, 21, 26, 28	0, 16, 23	7
O	8	3, 6, 12, 14, 20, 22, 27, 29	1, 17, 24	8
W	9	0, 4, 7, 13, 15, 21, 23, 28	2, 18, 25	9
N	10	1, 5, 8, 14, 16, 22, 24, 29	3, 19, 26	10
	11	0, 2, 6, 9, 15, 17, 23, 25	4, 20, 27	11
M	12	1, 3, 7, 10, 16, 18, 24, 26	5, 21, 28	12
O	13	2, 4, 8, 11, 17, 19, 25, 27	6, 22, 29	13
O	14	3, 5, 9, 12, 18, 20, 26, 28	0, 7, 23	14
N	15	4, 6, 10, 13, 19, 21, 27, 29	1, 8, 24	15
	16	0, 5, 7, 11, 14, 20, 22, 28	2, 9, 25	16
A	17	1, 6, 8, 12, 15, 21, 23, 29	3, 10, 26	17
G	18	0, 2, 7, 9, 13, 16, 22, 24	4, 11, 27	18
E	19	1, 3, 8, 10, 14, 17, 23, 25	5, 12, 28	19
	20	2, 4, 9, 11, 15, 18, 24, 26	6, 13, 29	20
D	21	3, 5, 10, 12, 16, 19, 25, 27	0, 7, 14	21
A	22	4, 6, 11, 13, 17, 20, 26, 28	1, 8, 15	22
Y	23	5, 7, 12, 14, 18, 21, 27, 29	2, 9, 16	23
	24	0, 6, 8, 13, 15, 19, 22, 28	3, 10, 17	24
	25	1, 7, 9, 14, 16, 20, 23, 29	4, 11, 18	25
	26	0, 2, 8, 10, 15, 17, 21, 24,	5, 12, 19	26
	27	1, 3, 9, 11, 16, 18, 22, 25	6, 13, 20	27
	28	2, 4, 10, 12, 17, 19, 23, 26	7, 14, 21	28
	29	3, 5, 11, 13, 18, 20, 24, 27	8, 15, 22	29

THE MOON THROUGH THE ZODIAC SIGNS

The following pages should offer a little insight into the way that the Moon's various sign positions might have a bearing on your day to day life, whatever your own Moon sign.

MOON IN ARIES TODAY

When the Moon is in Aries you should be looking to commence new ventures. This is a good time to get things on the move and make up your mind about a change in attitude. There is a possibility that you will not be at your most patient during these periods, though the great advantage of the Moon is that it never stays in the same place for very long. It would be fair to suggest that the Moon in Aries brings a tendency to be easily discouraged, and especially so if you are born into a part of the zodiac that gives you a natural desire to achieve a great deal in a short period of time.

MOON IN TAURUS TODAY

A very much more cautious position of the Moon this, and there is absolutely no point in trying to rush anything whilst the Moon occupies the zodiac sign of Taurus. This is a lunar position that suits the sort of individual who is a careful and considered actor on the stage of life and so can prove to be quite stultifying to the more dynamic signs. Good for all forms of creativity, for example getting cracking with home decorations or simply for painting a picture. The Moon in Taurus is also fairly useful for finance, but only if you are willing to look at long-term investments.

MOON IN GEMINI TODAY

This turns out to be a very good time for getting almost any sort of message across and especially so when it comes to explaining how your emotional nature is running. It should not be difficult to speak words of love whilst the Moon is in Gemini and you might also be in a good position to talk others round to a point of view that you have been personally holding for quite a while. At work you should be firing on all cylinders and can afford to back your own hunches just as long as you are willing to explain to those around you the way that your mind is working.

MOON IN CANCER TODAY

Some would say that this is the best position of all for the Moon, since it is at its most comfortable when resting in the watery sign of Cancer. Chances are that you will find yourself at your most sensitive during this short period and you might have to be just a little careful about the way that you put your message across to others. All the same it is likely that you would be able to make those closest to you understand your deepest feelings, so that words of love often pass to and fro whilst the Moon occupies this sign. The only real word of caution is that you could give offence without realising that you have done so.

MOON IN LEO TODAY

If you are the sort of individual who loves to preen yourself in public and who is not afraid to tell it how it really is, then you will be a fan of the Moon in Leo. Confidence is not likely to be lacking and you are able to get much done, whilst at the same time maintaining a happy and comfortable frame of mind. Most people are likely to understand what you are trying to say and you can afford to put on something of a show during times such as this. The Moon in Leo could make you more brave than you usually consider yourself to be and you should take the bull by the horns in projects that are important to you.

MOON IN VIRGO TODAY

Definitely a time for the fussy members of life and the Moon in Virgo tends to make most people look more carefully at all manner of projects in order to make certain that the details are sorted out properly. There could be delays and whilst they last it might be useful to get things running smoothly at home, since you are able to put the domestic message across much more easily whilst the Moon occupies this sign. Confidence may not appear to be all that high and yet it is likely that you will get far more done at this stage than you might expect. Following up on projects from the past is good now.

MOON IN LIBRA TODAY

If you have been thinking about forming a new friendship, or even a deeper sort of attachment, you could not find a better time for doing so than during those short periods during which the Moon occupies the sign of Libra. This is a period during which you will be at your most diplomatic, so it is unlikely that you would offer any offence, no matter how important it seems to be to speak your mind. Your general attitude is likely to be flexible and you can easily turn your mind around to appreciate a point of view which might not normally be your own. Artistic endeavours are well highlighted and you may find that your dress sense is especially good.

MOON IN SCORPIO TODAY

This tends to be a very deep sort of period and one during which you may be standing still for a while, taking stock of life and being willing to allow yourself the time you need to get to know yourself a great deal better. You might take things to heart more than would usually be the case and that means that you have to be careful to listen carefully and not to react too quickly. Remember that the Moon in Scorpio tends to make you feel more intense and that to many people such periods are only short in duration. Give and take in a family sense comes easily to you during such interludes.

MOON IN SAGITTARIUS TODAY

A time to lift your mind above the mundane and to think about matters that would usually tax your mind a little. You are quite philosophical during these periods and should be able to get things sorted out easily, probably with the help of others, since most people respond quite positively when the Moon occupies the sign of the Archer. Reaching for the impossible might not be a bad thing since you might at least be able to get half way towards your objectives and should end up fairly satisfied with your efforts. Comfort and security are not all that important and there could be a definite urge for fresh fields and pastures new.

MOON IN CAPRICORN TODAY

There is no point in advising a steady attitude whilst the Moon is in Capricorn because that comes as standard. You certainly will not find yourself in a position to take too many chances and it is significant to observe how cautious stock markets tend to be during the Moon's stay in Capricorn. However, this is a very good time for planning and for settling any details that need great attention, so that, as a planning period, this position of the Moon could turn out to be one of the most useful of all. Quick reactions would probably be a waste of time though, if you take hours out to think about life.

MOON IN AQUARIUS TODAY

How quickly things can change and this is certainly the case as the capricious Moon moves from Capricorn into Aquarius. You should find yourself to be much more dynamic, willing to back your hunches to the hilt and able to see through the fog of life, straight into the heart of almost any situation. The innovators of the world tend to enjoy this position of the Moon the best of all, so that if you have a particularly positive idea, this proves to be the best period of all to do something about it. Keep any tedious projects on hold and go out for what you really want in life. The very next breeze to come along could blow you towards your chosen destination and since you don't want to miss it, spread your sail and get moving.

MOON IN PISCES TODAY

Really coming to terms with almost anything can be rather difficult during those times when the Moon occupies the sign of Pisces, so this might not turn out to be the most dynamic period of the them all. It isn't hard to see how other people might be thinking and it would be fair to suggest that many individuals are slightly more likely to be intuitive with Pisces helping the situation. To use this position the best, you need to look carefully at the psychological profile of your family and friends because this is the time when you are liable to see clear through to their motives. Reaction time is slow and you probably won't want to move any mountains, though to compensate you will find that those around you are as understanding in their attitude as you probably tend to be yourself.

THE ASTRAL DIARY

How the diagrams work

Through the *picture diagrams* in the Astral Diary I want to help you to plot your year. With them you can see where the positive and negative aspects will be found each month. To make the most of them all you have to do is remember where and when!

Let me show you how they work . . .

THE MONTH AT A GLANCE

Just as there are twelve separate Zodiac Signs, so Astrologers believe that each sign has twelve separate aspects to life. Each of the twelve segments relates to a different personal aspect. I number and list them all every month as a key so that their meanings are always clear.

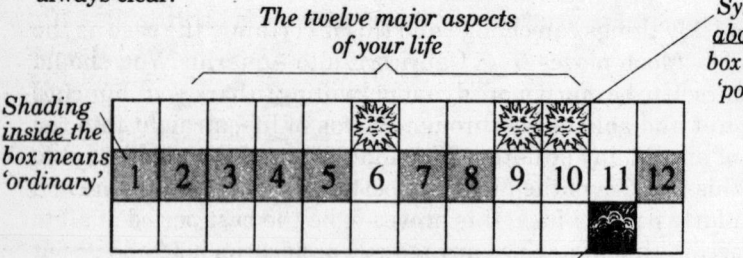

The twelve major aspects of your life

Symbols above the box means 'positive'

Shading inside the box means 'ordinary'

Symbol below the box means 'negative'

I have designed this chart to show you how and when these twelve different aspects are being influenced throughout the year. When the number rests comfortably in its shaded box, nothing out of the ordinary is to be expected. However, when a box turns white, then you should expect influences to become active in this area of your life. Where the influence is positive I have raised a smiling sun above its number. Where it is a negative, I hang a little rain cloud beneath it.

YOUR ENERGY RHYTHM CHART

On the opposite page is a picture diagram in which I am linking your zodiac group to the rhythm of the moon. In doing this I have calculated when you will be gaining strength from its influence and equally when you may be weakened by it.

If you think of yourself as being like the tides of the ocean then you may understand how your own energies must rise and fall too. And if you understand how it works and when it is working, then you can better organise your activities to achieve more and get things done more easily.

YOUR ENERGY-RHYTHM CHART

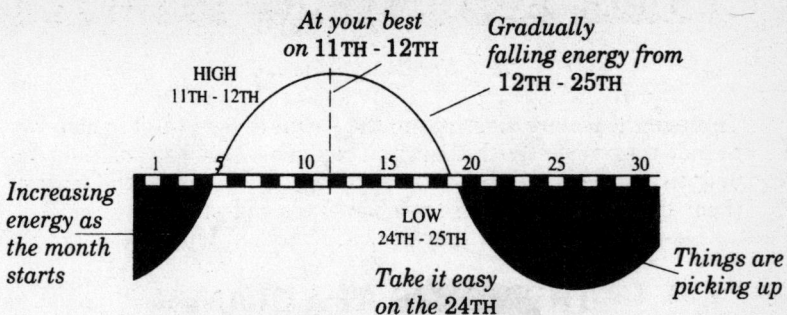

MOVING PICTURE SCREEN
Measured every week

LOVE, LUCK, MONEY & VITALITY

I hope that the diagram below offers more than a little fun. It is very easy to use. The bars move across the scale to give you some idea of the strength of opportunities open to you in each of the four areas. If LOVE stands at plus 4, then get out and put yourself about, because in terms of romance, things should be going your way. When the bar moves backwards then the opportunities are weakening and when it enters the negative scale, then romance should not be at the top of your list.

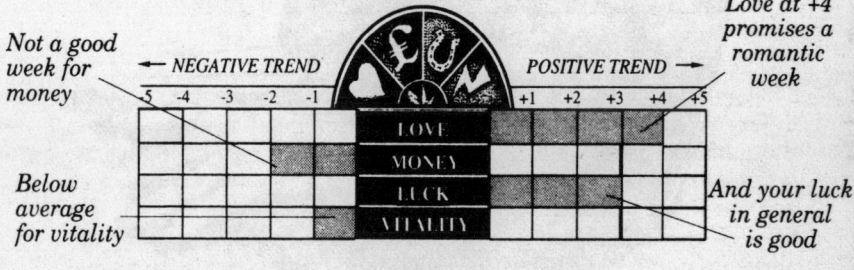

And Finally:

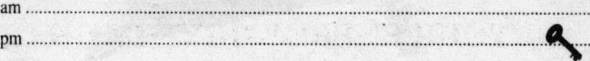

am ....

pm ....

The two lines that are left blank in each daily entry of the Astral Diary are for your own personal use. You may find them ideal for keeping a check on birthdays or appointments, though it could be an idea to make notes from the astrological trends and diagrams a few weeks in advance. Some of the lines carry a key, as above. These days are important because they indicate the working of 'astrological cycles' in your life. The key readings show how best you can act, react or simply work within them for greater success.

YOUR MONTH AT A GLANCE

The twelve numbered boxes represent the important areas in your life. The key to the numbers you will find beneath the panel. A sun above the number indicates that opportunities are around. A cloud below the number, that you should be a bit defensive. Nothing above or below and life will be pretty ordinary.

		☀				☀	☀				
1	2	3	4	5	6	7	8	9	10	11	12
				☁				☁			

KEY

1 Strength of Personality

2 Personal Finance

3 Useful Information Gathering

4 Domestic Affairs

5 Pleasure & Romance

6 Effective Work & Health

7 One to One Relationships

8 Questioning, Thinking & Deciding

9 External Influences / Education

10 Career Aspirations

11 Teamwork Activities

12 Unconscious Impulses

OCTOBER HIGHS AND LOWS

Here, I show how the rhythm of the Moon will affect you this month. Like the tide, your energies and abilities will rise and fall with its pattern. When it is above the date line, go-for-it. When it is below the line you should be resting.

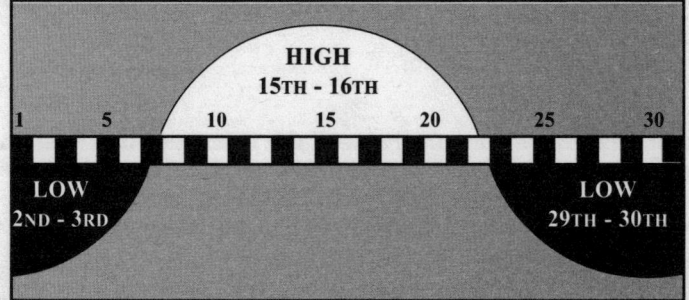

6 MONDAY
Moon Age Day 5 • Moon Sign Sagittarius

am..

pm..
You feel a definite need for mental stimulation and excitement. Social discussions go well and talks are positively highlighted, but do beware of appearing to know more than you do about any given situation. Other people are only too willing to catch you out and especially adversaries from the past.

7 TUESDAY
Moon Age Day 6 • Moon Sign Sagittarius

am..

pm..
Be as bold and brave as you know how to be. You find yourself at the start of a period which is more enterprising and which can be of tremendous importance to you. Perfect situations may not be exactly easy to come by, though even where there is adversity you should notice that your determination is really high.

8 WEDNESDAY
Moon Age Day 7 • Moon Sign Sagittarius

am..

pm..
You now ought to be well on top of most practical matters, but do need to feel that you are in control of your own affairs. Not a time for overtaxing yourself. Friends and particularly your partner, may require your personal touch in situations that have a bearing on their lives too.

9 THURSDAY
Moon Age Day 8 • Moon Sign Capricorn

am..

pm..
Points of disagreement are finely inevitable in emotional or relationship issues. At the very least this provides food for thought later on. Conversation is interesting and you will be doing your best to be honest and sincere about your real motivations in a day to day sense right now.

10 FRIDAY   *Moon Age Day 9 • Moon Sign Capricorn*

am ....

pm ....
Undoubtedly, there are power struggles somewhere in your vicinity and you would do well to avoid becoming involved in these. Certainly, this turns out to be a hard working day, but what you put into operation at this time could have significant consequences later on. This is a testing time.

11 SATURDAY   *Moon Age Day 10 •Moon Sign Aquarius*

am ....

pm ....
A friend or colleague may have some surprising favour for you. Progress with life, both in a personal and professional sense is easier and softer than has been the case recently. Good luck continues, though in the case of today it is probably you who is putting in the effort to tip the scales in your favour.

12 SUNDAY   *Moon Age Day 11 • Moon Sign Aquarius*

am ....

pm ....
It is all too easy now to challenge the opinions of others in a social setting or perhaps at home. This might be a mistake, since despite your verbal dexterity others could get the better of you. Appointments could be missed or delayed and there are general but unexpected hold-ups taking up some time.

← NEGATIVE TREND						POSITIVE TREND →				
-5	-4	-3	-2	-1		+1	+2	+3	+4	+5
					LOVE					
					MONEY					
					LUCK					
					VITALITY					

13 MONDAY
Moon Age Day 12 • Moon Sign Pisces

am . . . .

pm . . . .
Look out for some resistance to your plans or schemes as the working week gets underway. The opinions of other people don't always mesh with your own, and you might be a little more afraid to express yourself than would usually be the case. The pace of your everyday life quickens more than you expect.

14 TUESDAY
Moon Age Day 13 • Moon Sign Pisces

am . . . .

pm . . . .
Negotiations may benefit you in some way, provided that you are not expecting miraculous results at present. There are wide spread interests in your life and conversation proves to be especially stimulating. Aspects of love figure prominently in the lives of most Arians.

15 WEDNESDAY
Moon Age Day 14 • Moon Sign Aries

am . . . .

pm . . . .
Your spirits improve enormously as the Moon moves back into your own sign of Aries. Now you are out there in the mainstream of everyday life, and most objectives turn out as you would expect them to. This would be a good time to push your luck in some way and for getting what you want out of life, without effort.

16 THURSDAY
Moon Age Day 15 • Moon Sign Aries

am . . . .

pm . . . .
Now able to bring new plans into action, you can make significant progress with outstanding schemes and may be using today to plan carefully for the immediate future. If you are out and about, you can take the odd chance and gambles are more likely to pay off now. Definitely a time for getting things sorted out.

17 FRIDAY   *Moon Age Day 16 • Moon Sign Taurus*

am..

pm..
If you cling too stubbornly to your views today, you can make yourself
very unpopular with the individuals you have to mix with in a day to day
sense. A slightly tenuous aspect in your solar chart means you could be
out of favour with specific people at this time, and this in itself could lead
to conflict.

18 SATURDAY   *Moon Age Day 17 • Moon Sign Taurus*

am..

pm..
Your need for personal recreation could, if you are not careful, outweigh
work issues that are of primary importance. Professional involvements
should be looked at closely and are significant in the fact that you tend
to take important issues for granted. Look at things in a sensible
manner.

19 SUNDAY   *Moon Age Day 18 • Moon Sign Gemini*

am..

pm..
A good day when it comes to careful planning and to thinking about
things in a logical, yet progressive way. Although there could be a little
less fun in your social life, this is merely because you see your real
priorities in the practical world. Results tend to be achieved with
concentrated effort.

← *NEGATIVE TREND*   *POSITIVE TREND* →

-5	-4	-3	-2	-1			+1	+2	+3	+4	+5
					LOVE						
					MONEY						
					LUCK						
					VITALITY						

20 MONDAY   *Moon Age Day 19 • Moon Sign Gemini*

am ....

pm ....
Emotional assistance is called for by your partner, or possibly a close friend. However, be careful what you are willing to give, since what might be best for you possibly won't suit other people all that well. Financial issues need approaching with care, in which case solutions can be found quite quickly.

21 TUESDAY   *Moon Age Day 20 • Moon Sign Cancer*

am ....

pm ....
It isn't hard to judge how popular you are at the moment, but that is no real reason for allowing others to take advantage of your good nature. A pleasure trip with a loved one would be beneficial and in fact might work wonders, since your present optimism and cheerfulness is probably no more than skin deep.

22 WEDNESDAY   *Moon Age Day 21 • Moon Sign Cancer*

am ....

pm ....
Activities of any kind, and particularly those associated with hobbies or leisure pursuits tend to be going particularly well today. It is those areas of life that are undertaken through choice rather than through circumstance that are working out, whilst work demands more disciplined thinking.

23 THURSDAY   *Moon Age Day 22 • Moon Sign Cancer*

am ....

pm ....
Leisure pursuits and associations with others can fail to live up to your expectations in some way right now, especially where your partner is involved, or close personal friends. Part of the problem is that others do not share your enthusiasm or your point of view at present and you probably have to go it alone.

24 FRIDAY

Moon Age Day 23 • Moon Sign Leo

am...

pm...
Employers and superiors appear to be placing heavy demands upon you. If these take up a fair proportion of your free time, you probably have to look for the real difference between your priorities and the sense of obligation you feel towards yourself. Unrealistic demands should be left alone.

25 SATURDAY

Moon Age Day 24 • Moon Sign Leo

am...

pm...
It is now much easier to talk others into doing things your own way. Requests to figures of influence are likely to be granted if you have the courage to ask. This is a day when you should feel that all is right with the world at a time when it is possible to venture into new and interesting areas of life.

26 SUNDAY

Moon Age Day 25 • Moon Sign Virgo

am...

pm...
You feel a need to be close to your roots, to home and to family. A quieter period is in evidence, though plans and schemes still require that you keep up with recent developments. This being a Sunday, you may choose to get out and about later in the day, and can benefit from any decent weather that is still around.

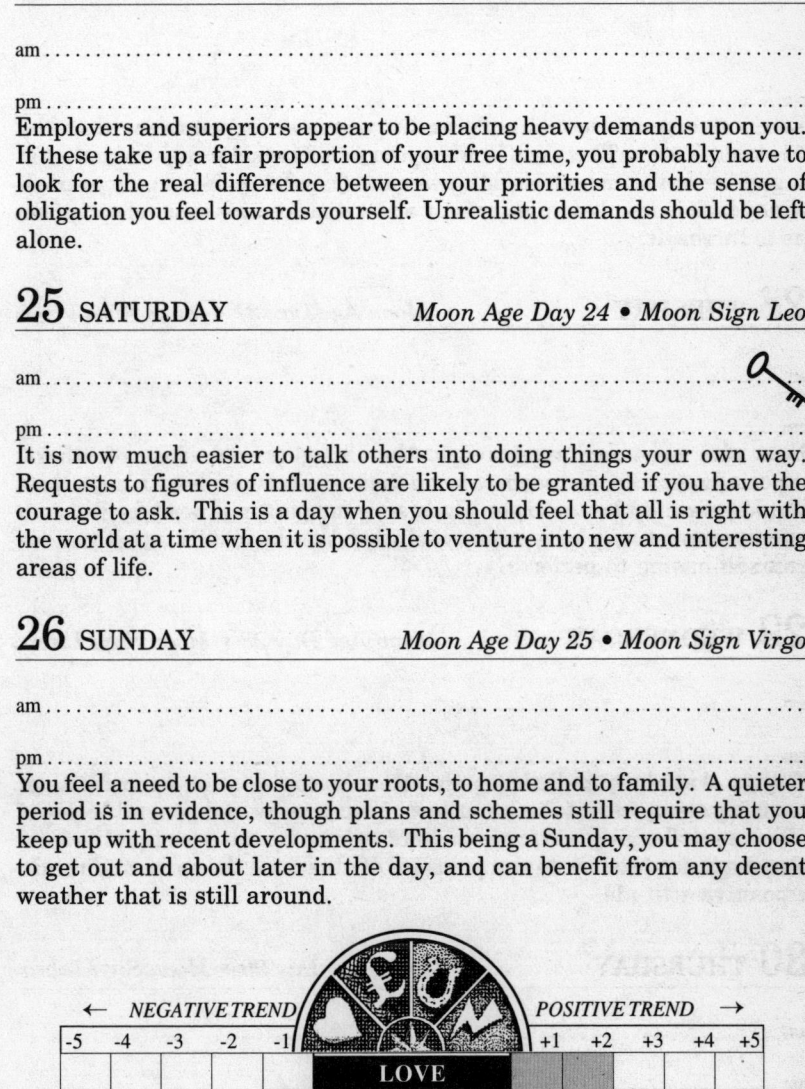

← NEGATIVE TREND								POSITIVE TREND →				
-5	-4	-3	-2	-1				+1	+2	+3	+4	+5
					LOVE							
					MONEY							
					LUCK							
					VITALITY							

27 MONDAY

Moon Age Day 26 • Moon Sign Virgo

am..

pm..
Fairly unexpected social calls and invitations crop up now that the
weekend is over. These can lighten your mood considerably and help you
to get the best from both worlds, work and friendship. You apply yourself
to any task in hand more cheerfully and with a greater sense of optimism
as to its result.

28 TUESDAY

Moon Age Day 27 • Moon Sign Virgo

am..

pm..
Now very open and receptive to the thoughts and ideas of others,
especially socially, you seem to be on their mental wavelength more than
would generally be the case. Even so, your personal need for freedom
and movement may have to go unfulfilled, thanks to duties that you see
yourself having to perform.

29 WEDNESDAY

Moon Age Day 28 • Moon Sign Libra

am..

pm..
Things slow down a little as the Moon occupies your opposite sign,
bringing along with it the lunar low. Your energy and general levels of
reserve are flagging and it seems hard to keep up the pace that life sets.
You don't need to bow to the pressure of others all the same and retain
a positive attitude.

30 THURSDAY

Moon Age Day 29 • Moon Sign Libra

am..

pm..
Some hold-ups come along to place pressure on general life progress. Try
to disregard their importance however even though it may feel that
everyone else is moving forward, leaving you standing still. In all
situations be yourself and look out for the help and support of loved ones
which is never very far away.

31 FRIDAY
Moon Age Day 0 • Moon Sign Scorpio

am...

pm...
It would be very easy for your partner to take your generosity for granted today, especially when it comes to money. You probably have to show yourself as being a little selfish in the pursuit of an individual objective, though this doesn't mean that you fail to assist other people on the way.

1 SATURDAY
Moon Age Day 1 • Moon Sign Scorpio

am...

pm...
Though relating socially is fulfilling this weekend, there is a possibility that you will be over-concerned about how others are feeling. Do your best to recognise the difference between pride in your appearance and personal vanity, which is fairly evident in you now. Saturday should be easygoing.

2 SUNDAY
Moon Age Day 2 • Moon Sign Scorpio

am...

pm...
You may be less confident than usual. Emotional issues are on your mind and may even cloud your judgement when it comes to important decisions which extend beyond house and home. It would be sensible to put these off until later and to turn your attention to less important matters which carry significant potential.

← NEGATIVE TREND						POSITIVE TREND →				
-5	-4	-3	-2	-1		+1	+2	+3	+4	+5
					LOVE					
					MONEY					
					LUCK					
					VITALITY					

1997

YOUR MONTH AT A GLANCE

The twelve numbered boxes represent the important areas in your life. The key to the numbers you will find beneath the panel. A sun above the number indicates that opportunities are around. A cloud below the number, that you should be a bit defensive. Nothing above or below and life will be pretty ordinary.

1	2	3	4	5	6	7	8	9	10	11	12

KEY

1 Strength of Personality
2 Personal Finance
3 Useful Information Gathering
4 Domestic Affairs
5 Pleasure & Romance
6 Effective Work & Health

7 One to One Relationships
8 Questioning, Thinking & Deciding
9 External Influences / Education
10 Career Aspirations
11 Teamwork Activities
12 Unconscious Impulses

NOVEMBER HIGHS AND LOWS

Here, I show how the rhythm of the Moon will affect you this month. Like the tide, your energies and abilities will rise and fall with its pattern. When it is above the date line, go-for-it. When it is below the line you should be resting.

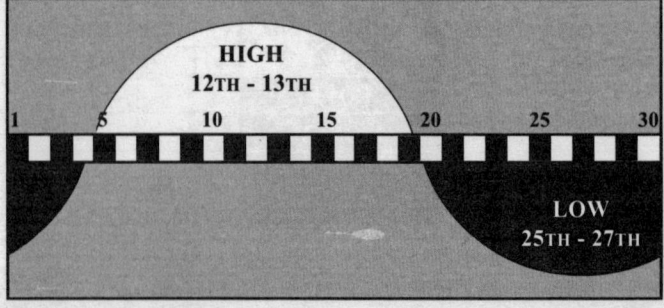

3 MONDAY   *Moon Age Day 3 • Moon Sign Sagittarius*

am . . . .

pm . . . .
The present ' off with the old and on with the new' phase continues and
the first Monday of the month probably brings you plenty to smile about.
However it is still sensible to remember that if something is not broken,
it probably does not need fixing. Some confusion at work is a possibility.

4 TUESDAY   *Moon Age Day 4 • Moon Sign Sagittarius*

am . . . .

pm . . . .
Avoid allowing yourself to fall into the trap of thinking that the grass is
greener on the other side of the fence, especially in a workaday sense.
The fact is that this is not the case. In many respects life should be going
well for you at present, and you need, once again, to avoid tampering too
much.

5 WEDNESDAY   *Moon Age Day 5 • Moon Sign Capricorn*

am . . . .

pm . . . .
With a new boost coming along to career developments, the middle of the
week almost certainly looks more enterprising and greater fun than
Monday or Tuesday could have been. You could be feeling excited over
a possible change of scene, or the chance to take on new and interesting
responsibilities at work.

6 THURSDAY   *Moon Age Day 6 • Moon Sign Capricorn*

am . . . .

pm . . . .
Today may bring along some very interesting challenges, and should
turn out to be a singularly important period when it comes to looking
back later in the month. Even relatively minor issues are working out
as you would wish and though you have to think on your feet this is not
a very difficult process for you.

7 FRIDAY
Moon Age Day 7 • Moon Sign Aquarius

am . . . .

pm . . . .
It might be difficult to tell if a good friend really does have your best interests at heart today, though chances are that this is the case and you may be inclined to react a little harshly at the moment. All in all you seem to be a rather sceptical Aries subject right now and need to lighten up somewhat.

8 SATURDAY
Moon Age Day 8 • Moon Sign Aquarius

am . . . .

pm . . . .
New and interesting mental stimulus comes in from the outside world, bringing a much brighter day and once that you should be pleased to call your own. Give and take in personal relationships also makes this a sphere that pleases you and at last you can get down to doing something really important.

9 SUNDAY
Moon Age Day 9 • Moon Sign Pisces

am . . . .

pm . . . .
Some confusion attends a great rise in your ego, probably as a result of things that other people are saying about you. There is no end to a constant stream of work, which Sunday does little to stem. Your comfort and security may seem to matter more now than would usually be the case but don't react too strongly.

NEGATIVE TREND ←						POSITIVE TREND →				
-5	-4	-3	-2	-1		+1	+2	+3	+4	+5
					LOVE					
					MONEY					
					LUCK					
					VITALITY					

10 MONDAY   *Moon Age Day 10 • Moon Sign Pisces*

am ....

pm ....
The influence of other people is clearly an important factor in your
working life at the beginning of this working week and you are probably
more inclined to listen to what they have to say now than might have
been the case during other periods. Few could dismiss your determination, or your abilities.

11 TUESDAY   *Moon Age Day 11 • Moon Sign Pisces*

am ....

pm ....
The best time of the month to put new plans into operation, with the
Moon about to pay it's monthly visit to your zodiac sign. Exactly why
things turn out the way they do may not be of that much interest to you
at present. All that really matters is that you have a great capacity to
make things happen.

12 WEDNESDAY   *Moon Age Day 12 • Moon Sign Aries*

am ....

pm ....
Energy comes to a peak and should make the middle of this week very
eventful and generally quite special. Even on those occasions when you
can do little or nothing to help your own life along, you are in there
pitching for others instead. For some Arians this could turn out to be a
memorable sort of day.

13 THURSDAY   *Moon Age Day 13 • Moon Sign Aries*

am ....

pm ....
Although this turns out to be a more 'business as usual' sort of day, than
some of the ones you have known recently, there is still plenty going for
you if you are willing to go out and look for it. Comfort and security come
low down your present list of priorities though such matters concern your
friends more.

14 FRIDAY
Moon Age Day 14 • Moon Sign Taurus

am ....

pm ....
Certain matters push their way towards a generally satisfying conclusion and you find that this Friday probably has a good deal going for it. Being in the right place at the right time can help you a lot and you can thank your own intuition for the ability. It is good to listen to your inner mind now.

15 SATURDAY
Moon Age Day 15 • Moon Sign Taurus

am ....

pm ....
Professional issues are less fulfilling now, though in the case of many this is probably only because you find yourself in a weekend mode. All the same this would be an ideal time to plan, even if putting some of your plans into action isn't possible Also a good interlude to think about a shopping spree.

16 SUNDAY
Moon Age Day 16 • Moon Sign Gemini

am ....

pm ....
There is little doubt that you can be especially persuasive at present, which means that you manage to get your own way in most matters that have a strong bearing on home and family. You might need to ring the changes socially because the last thing you would want to be at present is bored. Show some patience.

← NEGATIVE TREND						POSITIVE TREND →				
-5	-4	-3	-2	-1		+1	+2	+3	+4	+5
					LOVE					
					MONEY					
					LUCK					
					VITALITY					

17 MONDAY   *Moon Age Day 17 • Moon Sign Gemini*

am...

pm...
If your freedom seems to be rather curtailed as you embark on a new
working week, you can at least be more or less certain that you have the
ability to get on with a great deal of work. This fact may not please you
too much right now, but will be source of some satisfaction a little further
down the road.

18 TUESDAY   *Moon Age Day 18 • Moon Sign Cancer*

am...

pm...
A rather 'stay at home' phase is possible right now, and since you will
probably find this to be out of the question, you need to keep domestic
issues in your mind, no matter where you happen to be. Small worries
are put the back of your mind though and it is not likely that you will
react strongly to anything.

19 WEDNESDAY   *Moon Age Day 19 • Moon Sign Cancer*

am...

pm...
Most of the small changes to your personal life come from some fairly
unexpected directions at the moment and the majority of them turn out
to be far more interesting than you may expect. This is certainly no time
for becoming bored or for complaining that things are not working out
the way you would wish.

20 THURSDAY   *Moon Age Day 20 • Moon Sign Leo*

am...

pm...
You may feel a little pressured at work and if this turns out to be the case
it should be possible for you to help yourself by simply relaxing into
situations a bit more. Aries can become tense from time to time, but this
is not a helpful situation at all. Perhaps some sort of meditation might
be in order.

21 FRIDAY

Moon Age Day 21 • Moon Sign Leo

am . . . .

pm . . . .
Love and romance come centre stage in your life right now and there is
plenty to crow about when it comes down to feelings of personal success.
Whatever project you choose to give yourself to, undertake it with a
happy heart and a good spirit. A balanced time and one that should be
very enjoyable.

22 SATURDAY

Moon Age Day 22 • Moon Sign Leo

am . . . .

pm . . . .
As the Sun enters your solar ninth house, so you embark on a period that
should prove to be generally more rewarding when it comes to broaden-
ing your horizons. You are positively instructed to think big and not to
abandon any particular course of action unless you know for certain that
it cannot work out well.

23 SUNDAY

Moon Age Day 23 • Moon Sign Virgo

am . . . .

pm . . . .
A time when you could find that you are a little more self critical than is
really good for you. With plenty in the offing, and not all that much time
to get it all done you may have to pace yourself more than would usually
be the case. A greater level of dynamism is on the way, but patience now
counts.

						LOVE					
← *NEGATIVE TREND*							*POSITIVE TREND*	→		
-5	-4	-3	-2	-1			+1	+2	+3	+4	+5
					LOVE						
					MONEY						
					LUCK						
					VITALITY						

24 MONDAY   *Moon Age Day 24 • Moon Sign Virgo*

am...

pm...
People of influence, societies and groups of individuals look upon you
more favourably now and suit your present mentality. It is in these
directions that you need to look for support and you might be quite
surprised at what is actually on offer. Only take a little time out to listen
to what the world is saying.

25 TUESDAY   *Moon Age Day 25 • Moon Sign Libra*

am...

pm...
You are certainly best served at present by being willing to keep a low
profile and by refusing to push yourself any harder than you know to be
sensible. Get a particular job out of the way which has been bothering
you for a while and then you will feel more comfortable about committing
yourself in other ways.

26 WEDNESDAY   *Moon Age Day 26 • Moon Sign Libra*

am...

pm...
The lunar low is still around, and so it might be rather hard to make the
sort of progress that has been the case at other stages of this month. Not
everyone seems to have your best interests at heart it's true, though in
the main you should discover that there is some assistance on hand if you
need it.

27 THURSDAY   *Moon Age Day 27 • Moon Sign Libra*

am...

pm...
A day when you simply will not allow yourself to be confined, or when you
would be willing to accept second best from yourself, or anyone around
you. Keep up the pressure where you know it can make the most
difference to general trends and allow yourself the right to be correct
about something that others disagree with.

28 FRIDAY
Moon Age Day 28 • Moon Sign Scorpio

am ....

pm ....
In almost any race that you set yourself at present, you are inclined to win. Aries is not a sign that relishes coming second in any situation and you do have the sort of courage and tenacity at present that is the hallmark of your sign. Where positive actions fail to work out well for you, a little cheek comes to your aid.

29 SATURDAY
Moon Age Day 0 • Moon Sign Scorpio

am ....

pm ....
You are always busy and the fact the weekend comes along does little or nothing to slow down the general pace of life at present. You should be getting plenty out of personal relationships, with single Aries subjects having a particularly good period in store. Sort out some family papers now.

30 SUNDAY
Moon Age Day 1 • Moon Sign Sagittarius

am ....

pm ....
It would be fairest and best to keep to tried and tested paths where your endeavours are concerned this Sunday. It's possible that you will be happy to stay in or around your home and quite unlikely that you would be asking too much of yourself during this particular interlude of your active life.

← NEGATIVE TREND								POSITIVE TREND →			
-5	-4	-3	-2	-1			+1	+2	+3	+4	+5
					LOVE						
					MONEY						
					LUCK						
					VITALITY						

1997

YOUR MONTH AT A GLANCE

The twelve numbered boxes represent the important areas in your life. The key to the numbers you will find beneath the panel. A sun above the number indicates that opportunities are around. A cloud below the number, that you should be a bit defensive. Nothing above or below and life will be pretty ordinary.

1	2	3	4	5	6	7	8	9	10	11	12

2, 10, 11 have suns above; 7 has a cloud below

KEY

1 Strength of Personality
2 Personal Finance
3 Useful Information Gathering
4 Domestic Affairs
5 Pleasure & Romance
6 Effective Work & Health

7 One to One Relationships
8 Questioning, Thinking & Deciding
9 External Influences / Education
10 Career Aspirations
11 Teamwork Activities
12 Unconscious Impulses

DECEMBER HIGHS AND LOWS

Here, I show how the rhythm of the Moon will affect you this month. Like the tide, your energies and abilities will rise and fall with its pattern. When it is above the date line, go-for-it. When it is below the line you should be resting.

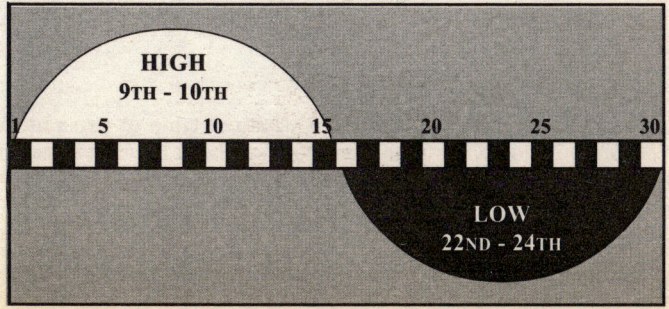

HIGH
9TH - 10TH

LOW
22ND - 24TH

1 MONDAY   *Moon Age Day 2 • Moon Sign Sagittarius*

am ....

pm ....
There should be a positive upturn to most situations at the start of December and you can expect general good luck to be on your side. Mercury is in an especially good position for you and this indicates better powers of communication, not to mention advantages coming your way as a result of things mechanical.

2 TUESDAY   *Moon Age Day 3 • Moon Sign Capricorn*

am ....

pm ....
In all probability you will decide that it is best to keep a low profile today. It isn't that anything particular is likely to be going wrong, merely that you think it best not to get involved in situations that are a little beyond your capabilities. Don't allow yourself to be pushed into anything at all.

3 WEDNESDAY   *Moon Age Day 4 • Moon Sign Capricorn*

am ....

pm ....
Though a socially pleasurable time, you may not find today to be of all that much use in a professional sense. If extra responsibilities regarding Christmas come upon you at this time, you should find that you have the hours to deal with them, even if others are not proving all that responsible now.

4 THURSDAY   *Moon Age Day 5 • Moon Sign Aquarius*

am ....

pm ....
Trying to please everyone is clearly a waste of time at present, all the more reason to get on with your own affairs, whilst leaving those around you alone more than usual in order that they can do the same. There are better financial trends about, some of which come about because of surprising situations.

5 FRIDAY   *Moon Age Day 6 • Moon Sign Aquarius*

am ....

pm ....
Various issues that you find yourself faced with today are probably not
half as important as you seem to be making them. Because of this it
would be sensible to let them take a back seat, whilst you enjoy yourself
socially and also let the rest of the world know what it is to have a truly
good time.

6 SATURDAY   *Moon Age Day 7 • Moon Sign Aquarius*

am ....

pm ....
Time spent on your own is not wasted today, even though there is no real
reason for you to withdraw. It is simply that there are occasions when
you want to think things through and this appears to be one of them.
Relatives and friends alike seem as though they are about to embark on
a very reasonable period.

7 SUNDAY   *Moon Age Day 8 • Moon Sign Pisces*

am ....

pm ....
The usual Arian assertiveness is definitely in evidence at the moment
and you would do well to curb such tendencies just a little if you can. All
the same, certain other people feel much more secure if it seems to them
that you are in charge. When mulling over professional matters, simply
wait and see.

← *NEGATIVE TREND*								*POSITIVE TREND* →					
-5	-4	-3	-2	-1			+1	+2	+3	+4	+5
					LOVE						
					MONEY						
					LUCK						
					VITALITY						

8 MONDAY ♦ *Moon Age Day 9 • Moon Sign Pisces*

am ....

pm ....
A good start to the week, primarily because before the end of today the
Moon is back in your own sign. The build-up to this event finds you
anxious to push forward in a number of ways. Limited speculation is
likely and you certainly have a greater degree of good luck on your side
at this time.

9 TUESDAY ♦ *Moon Age Day 10 • Moon Sign Aries*

am ....

pm ....
Things are still looking very good and you should find this to be one of
the very best days of the month for getting on well in a professional sense.
The chances are that you have great fortitude and that you will be
wanting to get certain matters sorted ahead of a fairly prolonged
Christmas period.

10 WEDNESDAY ♦ *Moon Age Day 11 • Moon Sign Aries*

am ....

pm ....
Today is stimulating, probably to the point of being exciting. In truth this
would probably be the very best day of the month if it were not for the
fact that you have a few difficult types to deal with along the way. The
attitude, even of loved ones, is a little difficult to understand and to deal
with now.

11 THURSDAY ♦ *Moon Age Day 12 • Moon Sign Taurus*

am ....

pm ....
Practical work issues show a great deal of progress today and you should
soon see that the minor obstacles that stood around you yesterday are
now being well and truly removed. A good time for speaking your mind,
though less so in a personal sense, because you could easily upset
someone you care for deeply.

12 FRIDAY ♦ *Moon Age Day 13 • Moon Sign Taurus*

am . . . .

pm . . . .
Not a day to allow yourself to feel down in the mouth about anything, even though to do so would be very easy at present. Looking ahead, you probably don't see the degree of excitement that you would really care for, so that life appears to be all work and responsibility. You should soon feel different.

13 SATURDAY ♦ *Moon Age Day 14 • Moon Sign Gemini*

am . . . .

pm . . . .
Someone appears to be trying to get into your good books and to be quite honest it would be fairly sensible not to interfere with this process. These trends seem to work towards your own personal agenda very well indeed and you have a great ability to get on with just about anyone at the present time.

14 SUNDAY ♦ *Moon Age Day 15 • Moon Sign Gemini*

am . . . .

pm . . . .
Travel arrangements may be subject to a few upsets and if so all you can really do is to put up with a little inconvenience and do your best to work around things as much as possible. Getting everything sorted out in a day to day sense could well mean having to call on the help or advice of a good friend.

← NEGATIVE TREND							POSITIVE TREND →			
-5	-4	-3	-2	-1		+1	+2	+3	+4	+5
					LOVE					
					MONEY					
					LUCK					
					VITALITY					

15 MONDAY ♦ *Moon Age Day 16 • Moon Sign Cancer*

am ....

pm ....
Things probably feel almost perfect at present, though not quite. If anything, it is the niggles of life that get on your nerves at present, even though there is no real reason for this. You can't get away from such trends and so all you can really do is to work within them. A clear view of the future becomes possible.

16 TUESDAY ♦ *Moon Age Day 17 • Moon Sign Cancer*

am ....

pm ....
You are clearly trying to do your best for almost everyone you come across at the moment, even if they do not always realise the fact for themselves. A little of this and a bit of that is the way to proceed at the moment because you would soon get tired of doing the same old things time and again.

17 WEDNESDAY ♦ *Moon Age Day 18 • Moon Sign Leo*

am ....

pm ....
Although you might find yourself subject to a few restrictions early on today, in the main you have a positive and assertive time in front of you. The middle of the week offers better chances at work, whilst the greatest blessing of the day is the sheer volume of work that you can actually get through.

18 THURSDAY ♦ *Moon Age Day 19 • Moon Sign Leo*

am ....

pm ....
If everything seems a bit of a race you now find yourself faced with a day when you can slow things down and find the space and place that you really need in order to think things through. There are people around who are willing to take some of the strain, and you are only to willing to go along with them.

19 FRIDAY   ♦   *Moon Age Day 20 • Moon Sign Leo*

am ....

pm ....
You should be in a real position of influence today and look favourably upon those people who are in the very best position to work on your behalf. This is a regular theme this month, but probably never more so than today. You are willing to take what life offers, though most of it should look pretty good now.

20 SATURDAY   ♦   *Moon Age Day 21 • Moon Sign Virgo*

am ....

pm ....
You seem to be exhibiting a vague sense of wanderlust. which might turn out to be rather a puzzle, both to yourself and to others that you have to deal with today. Don't allow minor hiccups to get in the way and do what you can to get plans for Christmas totally sorted out ahead of the period itself.

21 SUNDAY   ♦   *Moon Age Day 22 • Moon Sign Virgo*

am ....

pm ....
Hedged in by all sorts of little things, it is likely that you are not feeling on top form today. The only way to deal with such trends is to work through them as steadily as you can. There should be no shortage of advice about, but are you really in the right frame of mind to listen to what others are saying?

← *NEGATIVE TREND*							*POSITIVE TREND* →			
-5	-4	-3	-2	-1		+1	+2	+3	+4	+5
					LOVE					
					MONEY					
					LUCK					
					VITALITY					

22 MONDAY ♦ *Moon Age Day 23 • Moon Sign Libra*

am . . . .

pm . . . .
Venus is very strong for you at the moment, so that generally speaking
you are certainly on a winning streak. Love especially plays an
important part in your life and for the first time this month you might
actually realise that Christmas is just around the corner. It's time to sit
back and let life help you out.

23 TUESDAY ♦ *Moon Age Day 24 • Moon Sign Libra*

am . . . .

pm . . . .
Most likely this is a final chance to sit back and allow life to pass you by,
before you launch yourself into a very protracted, though definitely
positive sort of time in the days to come. You have the lunar low to deal
with now and it is this planetary influence that finds you being rather
quiet.

24 WEDNESDAY ♦ *Moon Age Day 25 • Moon Sign Libra*

am . . . .

pm . . . .
Your ego is very strong, so much so that you are more than willing to say
what you think to almost anyone you come across. This being Christmas
Eve, you will want to get necessary duties out of the way as soon as
possible, leaving the maximum time for helping with the last minute
details this evening.

25 THURSDAY ♦ *Moon Age Day 26 • Moon Sign Scorpio*

am . . . .

pm . . . .
It's a good Christmas Day and might seem like fun and games all the
way. Most of the people you care about the most should be with you at
some stage and although you allow yourself very little time to watch
what is going on around you, there is more than a little excitement at
your disposal on this day.

26 FRIDAY ♦ *Moon Age Day 27 • Moon Sign Scorpio*

am..

pm..
Although it is easier to make new social contacts today, the truth is that
you might choose not to do so. The actions and decisions of the people
you deal with in a family sense could make this a somewhat surprising,
though eventful sort of Boxing Day. Not a time for hedging your bets all
that much.

27 SATURDAY *Moon Age Day 28 • Moon Sign Sagittarius*

am..

pm..
You should be on the receiving end of some fairly happy news before
today is out. It is likely that you now find yourself with a little more time
on your hands to do those things which have had to wait during the
busier times lately. There should also be a few moments to really look
at Christmas gifts.

28 SUNDAY *Moon Age Day 29 • Moon Sign Sagittarius*

am..

pm..
A slight clash of personality between yourself and other people who are
equally strong by nature is not out of the question at this time. Keep
things on a less than personal footing if you can and try not to allow
yourself to go over the top. The best action of all would be to avoid
arguments altogether.

← *NEGATIVE TREND*							*POSITIVE TREND* →			
-5	-4	-3	-2	-1		+1	+2	+3	+4	+5
					LOVE					
					MONEY					
					LUCK					
					VITALITY					

29 MONDAY *Moon Age Day 0 • Moon Sign Sagittarius*

am ....

pm ....
Spending a little time with your family could prove to be the most
rewarding possibility of this most useful and interesting today. You can't
be responsible for the actions of others but should have good enough
reason to be proud of them at the moment. Get your New Year resolu-
tions sorted out as soon as possible.

30 TUESDAY *Moon Age Day 1 • Moon Sign Capricorn*

am ....

pm ....
A most satisfactory day from most points of view though probably a little
restricting in a professional sense. This might be due to the fact that you
are not back at work yet and therefore cannot really have any say in
matters practical. Hold hard for a day or two and realise that you can
act a little later.

31 WEDNESDAY *Moon Age Day 2 • Moon Sign Capricorn*

am ....

pm ....
If it suddenly dawns on you that this is the last day of the year, you might
find yourself somewhat out on a limb in a social sense. However, it is
more likely that someone close to you has plans and that these will be put
into operation on your behalf. Sit back and watch the sands of another
year run on.

1 THURSDAY *Moon Age Day 3 • Moon Sign Aquarius*

am ....

pm ....
A generally bright and happy start to the year with plenty to play for and
life going your way most of the time. You may not be able to have
absolutely everything you want today but even where you can't you are
willing to make do and mend. Love is on the cards for some Aries
subjects, make sure you are one of them.

2 FRIDAY
Moon Age Day 4 • Moon Sign Aquarius

am ....

pm ....
The everyday concerns of life are apt to get you down more than they probably should, though this does little to prevent you moving upward and onward in a career sense. An idea that you have ages ago might have been forgotten by you, though others still remember your inspiration and call it into play.

3 SATURDAY
Moon Age Day 5 • Moon Sign Pisces

am ....

pm ....
Out and about in the big wide world, you manage to make a generally favourable impression wherever you go. Get any tedious jobs out of the way as early in the day as you can and save the later part of Saturday for pleasing yourself. Probably not a time for very practical jobs, most of which can wait.

4 SUNDAY
Moon Age Day 6 • Moon Sign Pisces

am ....

pm ....
Relax in the bosom of your family and keep out of the cold winter weather if you get the chance. This would be a good day to curl up in front of the television or for looking out a good book that you have been meaning to read for ages. There is little space for anxiety inside you at present.

-5	-4	-3	-2	-1	+1	+2	+3	+4	+5
					LOVE				
				MONEY					
				LUCK					
				VITALITY					

← *NEGATIVE TREND* *POSITIVE TREND* →

1998
YOUR MONTH AT A GLANCE

The twelve numbered boxes represent the important areas in your life. The key to the numbers you will find beneath the panel. A sun above the number indicates that opportunities are around. A cloud below the number, that you should be a bit defensive. Nothing above or below and life will be pretty ordinary.

1	2 ☀	3 ☀	4	5	6 ☁	7 ☁	8	9	10 ☀	11	12

KEY

1 Strength of Personality
2 Personal Finance
3 Useful Information Gathering
4 Domestic Affairs
5 Pleasure & Romance
6 Effective Work & Health

7 One to One Relationships
8 Questioning, Thinking & Deciding
9 External Influences / Education
10 Career Aspirations
11 Teamwork Activities
12 Unconscious Impulses

JANUARY HIGHS AND LOWS

Here, I show how the rhythm of the Moon will affect you this month. Like the tide, your energies and abilities will rise and fall with its pattern. When it is above the date line, go-for-it. When it is below the line you should be resting.

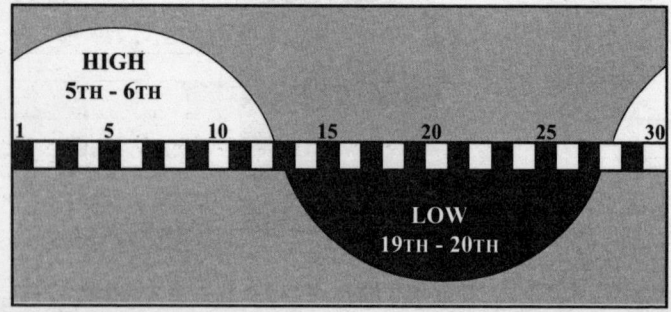

HIGH
5TH - 6TH

LOW
19TH - 20TH

5 MONDAY   *Moon Age Day 7 • Moon Sign Aries*

am ....

pm ....

Having fully refreshed yourself you should now be ready for almost anything that the new week throws at you. The Moon is in your sign and there is everything to play for in a practical sense. Money matters can be resolved now and most Aries types will notice that general good luck is around.

6 TUESDAY   *Moon Age Day 8 • Moon Sign Aries*

am ....

pm ....

It's time for a clean sweep, no matter what area of your life you choose to look at right now. There are people around who are only too willing to follow your lead, and who will be keen to get cracking with all sorts of new possibilities. Even these dynamic types will find it hard to keep up with you.

7 WEDNESDAY   *Moon Age Day 9 • Moon Sign Taurus*

am ....

pm ....

There are occasions when you take so much on that you cannot fail to tire yourself on the way. It isn't the physical demands that get you down so much as the level of anxiety of which you are capable. Sometimes it is sensible to sit back and realise how stressed you are. Then you can jettison the load.

8 THURSDAY   *Moon Age Day 10 • Moon Sign Taurus*

am ....

pm ....

Routines would certainly get you down at the moment, which is why you opt for as much change and diversity as you can manage to cram into your life. The self assessment of yesterday did not last too long, but it's hard to keep and Aries person down and you are no exception.

9 FRIDAY
Moon Age Day 11 • Moon Sign Gemini

am . . . .

pm . . . .

Even the most casual conversation can offer you a wealth of new ideas right now and you are certainly not stuck for something to say or do at the right time today. People of every imaginable type come into your life and bring with them a breath of fresh air that is never out of place for you personally.

10 SATURDAY
Moon Age Day 12 • Moon Sign Gemini

am . . . .

pm . . . .

Have a crack at something that you have not done before. This probably does not mean taking up rock climbing of para-gliding, though of course if this is really what takes your fancy - why not? In the main it is your personal life that comes in for a little close scrutiny, and you will not be found lacking.

11 SUNDAY
Moon Age Day 13 • Moon Sign Gemini

am . . . .

pm . . . .

If there is the odd unpleasant job to get out of the way today you would be well advised to get it done as early as you can. Most of Sunday responds to what you wish to do personally and you won't lack any number of new incentives if you choose to look for them. Keep an open mind about possible changes at home.

← *NEGATIVE TREND*								*POSITIVE TREND*	→	
-5	-4	-3	-2	-1		+1	+2	+3	+4	+5
					LOVE					
					MONEY					
					LUCK					
					VITALITY					

70

12 MONDAY   *Moon Age Day 14 • Moon Sign Cancer*

am ....

pm ....

You cannot afford to waste a single minute at the start of this Monday and may well be rushed off your feet from the start of the day until its end. It would be sensible to allow someone else to take some of the stress and strain, though knowing what sort of a person you are this may not be likely.

13 TUESDAY   *Moon Age Day 15 • Moon Sign Cancer*

am ....

pm ....

It is likely that you still have not learned that there is no reason for you to do absolutely everything yourself. The problem is that although you care very deeply for many of the people around you, it does not seem to you that they are half as capable as you are. Today you might be in for a shock.

14 WEDNESDAY   *Moon Age Day 16 • Moon Sign Leo*

am ....

pm ....

Certainly not a day for hiding your talents. There are plenty of opportunities to show the world that you know what you are talking about in some specialised sense and you need to stick to your own thing right now. If others shocked you yesterday, the favour is returned in fine measure now.

15 THURSDAY   *Moon Age Day 17 • Moon Sign Leo*

am ....

pm ....

Be brave if you have a dental appointment or if you must go and see the boss. You are far more courageous at present than you feel yourself to be, though even Aries subjects can get the odd butterfly now and again. A good day for forward planning and on which to lay out a new plan of action.

16 FRIDAY

Moon Age Day 18 • Moon Sign Virgo

am ....

pm ....

Not everyone can force situations through in quite the way that you can. Perhaps this is a good thing because you are going to learn that a gentle touch can get things done every bit as well on occasions. Beware of bargains that seem too good to be true. There is every chance that they are a con.

17 SATURDAY

Moon Age Day 19 • Moon Sign Virgo

am ....

pm ....

The strange, the weird and the wonderful all have a part to play in your thinking and your life today. Bigger and better things wait around every corner, the only trouble being that you do not have a periscope and so have to rely on your intuition. In most cases this is unlikely to let you down.

18 SUNDAY

Moon Age Day 20 • Moon Sign Virgo

am ....

pm ....

Take a break from the regular and make Sunday be what you would wish. You do not always have to go with the flow, as you are only too well aware. This is a day for allowing others to follow your lead, which in the main they should be quite willing to do. All in all this should be a contented day.

← *NEGATIVE TREND*						*POSITIVE TREND* →				
-5	-4	-3	-2	-1		+1	+2	+3	+4	+5
					LOVE					
					MONEY					
					LUCK					
					VITALITY					

19 MONDAY

Moon Age Day 21 • Moon Sign Libra

am ....

pm ....

Aries through the looking glass! Today you are forced to take a long, hard look at some of the things you appear to be to the rest of the world. Although this is no bad thing, in one or two ways it might shock you somewhat. Never mind, you always end up realising what a really together person you are.

20 TUESDAY

Moon Age Day 22 • Moon Sign Libra

am ....

pm ....

A period for remembering some of the multitude of favours that have come to you from others, and during which you can return one or two of them. Not that this is a difficult procedure because you are in the right frame of mind to benefit from them yourself. What a resourceful person you can be.

21 WEDNESDAY

Moon Age Day 23 • Moon Sign Scorpio

am ....

pm ....

Don't expect everything to go your way right now. The Moon is in your opposite sign and no matter how much you would wish to get ahead, it looks as though this is just not going to be possible. Slow and steady progress does not suit you very well but is certainly the best thing at present.

22 THURSDAY

Moon Age Day 24 • Moon Sign Scorpio

am ....

pm ....

You are tough and resilient, but that does not mean that you can go it alone all the time. While the lunar low is around why not take advantage of the many offers that come from family and friends? The truth is that they are more than willing to put themselves out on your behalf, even if that means convincing you of their sincerity.

23 FRIDAY
Moon Age Day 25 • Moon Sign Scorpio

am . . . .

pm . . . .

The most repressive qualities of the lunar low are now left behind you and you can at least plan for the more progressive phase that lies ahead. Of course this may not be all that easy on a Friday and it is true that your level of energy is not high. Why not opt instead for a slight change to your social life?

24 SATURDAY
Moon Age Day 26 • Moon Sign Sagittarius

am . . . .

pm . . . .

This should be a good and enjoyable Saturday, with everything to play for in a social and a romantic sense and plenty of people around to tell you how wonderful you really are. In the main what they are saying is quite true, and what really sets today apart is that you manage to believe them.

25 SUNDAY
Moon Age Day 27 • Moon Sign Sagittarius

am . . . .

pm . . . .

You certainly will not like yourself as much today as you did yesterday. This will be especially true if you have to take someone to task for not pulling their weight. Nevertheless you do sometimes have to be just a little cruel to be kind and the person concerned should thank you enough later on.

← NEGATIVE TREND						POSITIVE TREND →				
-5	-4	-3	-2	-1		+1	+2	+3	+4	+5
					LOVE					
					MONEY					
					LUCK					
					VITALITY					

26 MONDAY   *Moon Age Day 28 • Moon Sign Capricorn*

am ....

pm ....

There are certain alterations to routines that will not suit you at all, even though you hate to be tied down in any case. In some spheres of your life you are mixing with a rough and ready lot and will not have full control of your own destiny. There could be some excitement in riding the white water of life.

27 TUESDAY   *Moon Age Day 29 • Moon Sign Capricorn*

am ....

pm ....

Don't try to keep up with the Jones' because half the time what they have is not for you in any case. Instead be content to plough your own furrow and to make certain that all your plans have a sensible base and a positive incentive. This is not at all hard, especially with loved ones to help you out.

28 WEDNESDAY   *Moon Age Day 0 • Moon Sign Aquarius*

am ....

pm ....

Since you are going up greatly in your own estimation you can expect to feel quite content with your progress and your present attitude. This does not mean allowing yourself to be smug, but there are times when you genuinely do deserve to award yourself a pat on the back. This is such a time.

29 THURSDAY   *Moon Age Day 1 • Moon Sign Aquarius*

am ....

pm ....

Personalities of every imaginable description could turn up in your life at the moment and it would be fair to suggest that you have an able and capable attitude right now. Enjoyment of a personal sort is very important today and you set out to make certain that the people you love enjoy life as much as you can.

30 FRIDAY

Moon Age Day 2 • Moon Sign Pisces

am ....

pm ....

As entertaining as can be, you manage to make Friday very much your own. Any tedious aspects of life are put on one side for the moment as you whistle a little tune to yourself more or less right through the day. A tendency to feel a little tired only goes to prove how busy you have been recently.

31 SATURDAY

Moon Age Day 3 • Moon Sign Pisces

am ....

pm ....

The last day of January brings a Saturday of some surprises. Not all of them seem to be what you would wish at first, though it should become obvious later on that the majority of them are designed to make your life better eventually. You manage to smile at the most ridiculous situations.

1 SUNDAY

Moon Age Day 4 • Moon Sign Aries

am ....

pm ....

It does not really matter if you managed to remember to say 'White Rabbits' today, because the lunar high is more or less certain to offer a positive and happy start to February. Lady Luck is with you and it looks as though you can afford to take the odd chance with life. Happiness is of a personal sort.

← *NEGATIVE TREND*							*POSITIVE TREND*	→		
-5	-4	-3	-2	-1		+1	+2	+3	+4	+5
					LOVE					
					MONEY					
					LUCK					
					VITALITY					

1998

YOUR MONTH AT A GLANCE

The twelve numbered boxes represent the important areas in your life. The key to the numbers you will find beneath the panel. A sun above the number indicates that opportunities are around. A cloud below the number, that you should be a bit defensive. Nothing above or below and life will be pretty ordinary.

1	2	3 ☀	4	5	6	7	8 ☀	9	10	11	12 ☀
				☁	☁						

KEY

1 Strength of Personality
2 Personal Finance
3 Useful Information Gathering
4 Domestic Affairs
5 Pleasure & Romance
6 Effective Work & Health

7 One to One Relationships
8 Questioning, Thinking & Deciding
9 External Influences / Education
10 Career Aspirations
11 Teamwork Activities
12 Unconscious Impulses

FEBRUARY HIGHS AND LOWS

Here, I show how the rhythm of the Moon will affect you this month. Like the tide, your energies and abilities will rise and fall with its pattern. When it is above the date line, go-for-it. When it is below the line you should be resting.

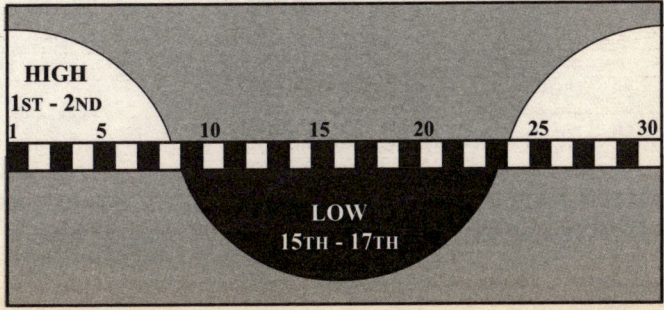

2 MONDAY   *Moon Age Day 5 • Moon Sign Aries*

am . . . .

pm . . . .

You need a change of scenery and an altered routine as much as you can manage today. This is a time when you can very easily become bored and you would not be helped at all by staying to expected courses of action. It would do certain other people a lot of good if they had to think things through.

3 TUESDAY   *Moon Age Day 6 • Moon Sign Taurus*

am . . . .

pm . . . .

At least for the first part of the day it would be sensible to concentrate on one thing at once. It's important to keep your eye on the ball when it comes to dealing with new professional projects and you may be asked to take on a degree of new responsibility. This should not phase you in the slightest.

4 WEDNESDAY   *Moon Age Day 7 • Moon Sign Taurus*

am . . . .

pm . . . .

Look out for a little excitement coming into your life at the moment. There are gains to be made at work for many of you, mainly because others are coming round to your point of view at last. This is no time to be pushing specific issues however since most of them come good of their own accord.

5 THURSDAY   *Moon Age Day 8 • Moon Sign Taurus*

am . . . .

pm . . . .

Realising what you have to be grateful for it is likely that you will be showing a great deal of support for family members. You are also in an excellent position to offer some sort of help to a friend who seems to be in special need right now. Entertainment is on the cards by the evening.

6 FRIDAY   *Moon Age Day 9 • Moon Sign Gemini*

am ....

pm ....

A rare opportunity to do something that really takes your fancy could cause you to ignore more practical matters early in the day. You need space to think about personal matters and there is just the slight chance that you feel rather crowded by people and circumstances at present. This feeling does not last.

7 SATURDAY   *Moon Age Day 10 • Moon Sign Gemini*

am ....

pm ....

If you deliberately set out to shock certain people this weekend you should not be surprised if they react accordingly. Perhaps you are not realising what a high profile you tend to have and that makes it rather awkward to assess the impact of your dominant Aries nature. Confidence is not lacking at all.

8 SUNDAY   *Moon Age Day 11 • Moon Sign Cancer*

am ....

pm ....

A quieter day than you may have been expecting, bearing in mind what yesterday tended to be like. This would be an ideal time for getting your thinking head on regarding a project that has had to take a back seat for quite some time. Getting your own way in a domestic sense is not at all difficult now.

← *NEGATIVE TREND*						*POSITIVE TREND* →				
-5	-4	-3	-2	-1		+1	+2	+3	+4	+5
					LOVE					
					MONEY					
					LUCK					
					VITALITY					

9 MONDAY
Moon Age Day 12 • Moon Sign Cancer

am . . . .

pm . . . .

A red letter day for most Aries subjects and in many ways an ideal start to the working week. With everything to play for and plenty of people willing to take your ideas at face value this is no time to be hiding your light under a bushel. Get out there into the mainstream of life and show what you can do.

10 TUESDAY
Moon Age Day 13 • Moon Sign Leo

am . . . .

pm . . . .

Whilst other people go round and round in circles you are especially busy proving that once you have made your mind up about a particular course of action you will not be held back. This is the side of your nature that certain people find difficult to deal with. You may even scare them a little.

11 WEDNESDAY
Moon Age Day 14 • Moon Sign Leo

am . . . .

pm . . . .

Even when you are in a situation that is not all that clear to you it would be sensible to act as if you knew very well what you were doing. This way you can fool the whole world into thinking that you are just as confident as always. There is every chance that you will also fool yourself on the way.

12 THURSDAY
Moon Age Day 15 • Moon Sign Leo

am . . . .

pm . . . .

Creating the right atmosphere for loving relationships to develop and grow is what you are all about today. There could be a slight lull in practical matters and you will need something to focus your energies on. For some Aries subjects this is a time of important new starts and positive changes.

13 FRIDAY   *Moon Age Day 16 • Moon Sign Virgo*

am . . . .

pm . . . .

Although this is Friday the thirteenth you may have little enough time to register the fact until much later in the day. Be certain that you can have what you want and you are half way to achieving it. All the same it might be rather awkward proving to other people that this is genuinely the case.

14 SATURDAY   *Moon Age Day 17 • Moon Sign Virgo*

am . . . .

pm . . . .

Relaxing isn't always easy, though the imminent arrival of the lunar low does at least offer you the chance to give it a try. Being naturally quieter than usual, you are going to have to show those around you that you are not sulking about anything, mainly because you have been so chatty during the last few days.

15 SUNDAY   *Moon Age Day 18 • Moon Sign Libra*

am . . . .

pm . . . .

Another fairly quiet time but not a period when you want to do all that much in any case. You should be happy to sit and watch life go by a fact that will surprise your relatives and friends far more than it does you. Being naturally inclined to learn from past happenings you are more contemplative than usual.

| ← NEGATIVE TREND | | | | | | POSITIVE TREND → | | | | |
-5	-4	-3	-2	-1		+1	+2	+3	+4	+5
					LOVE					
					MONEY					
					LUCK					
					VITALITY					

16 MONDAY
Moon Age Day 19 • Moon Sign Libra

am . . . .

pm . . . .

A normal response to just about any situation is much less likely that usual right now. Preparing for another busy period that lies just around the corner you should be more than happy to immerse yourself in a mass of plans and ideas. Not everyone appears to have your best interests at heart.

17 TUESDAY
Moon Age Day 20 • Moon Sign Libra

am . . . .

pm . . . .

You are back in gear and fully on the move again, thanks to some fairly startling influences in your solar chart right now. It's time to take the bull by the horns in the way that your sign can do better than any other. Such a high profile demands that you think on your feet, though this is not hard for you.

18 WEDNESDAY
Moon Age Day 21 • Moon Sign Scorpio

am . . . .

pm . . . .

It is the things that other people do not see about you that count for the most at present because this is how you manage to take the world by surprise. Most of the time you are fully committed to looking after the whole world and his dog, whereas you manage to find time now to please yourself.

19 THURSDAY
Moon Age Day 22 • Moon Sign Scorpio

am . . . .

pm . . . .

Doing the right thing is not difficult as far as you are concerned, though it might be rather difficult to prove to others that this is what is really going on. In a romantic sense you know what you expect from your partner and it might be worth having a quiet word to ensure that they agree.

20 FRIDAY
Moon Age Day 23 • Moon Sign Sagittarius

am..

pm..

It should be fairly easy to pace yourself and at least that way you do not wear yourself out too early in the day. With an extra helping of luck coming your way at present you can afford to take a chance of two. This is not really the case in personal relationships however, which take careful handling.

21 SATURDAY
Moon Age Day 24 • Moon Sign Sagittarius

am..

pm..

Whilst those around you are running out of steam you tend to be fairly certain that you can keep going, no matter what. This makes for an interesting day, even if you have to take most of the strain. This really does not matter as long as you are happy, which appears to be the case at present.

22 SUNDAY
Moon Age Day 25 • Moon Sign Capricorn

am..

pm..

You would really appreciate a quiet sort of Sunday, but it looks unlikely that this will turn out to be the case. Not that it really matters in the end because you are definitely in the right mood to take things as they come. Gains are there to be made in a domestic sense, whilst personal attachments look very secure.

← *NEGATIVE TREND*　　　　　　　　　　*POSITIVE TREND* →

-5	-4	-3	-2	-1			+1	+2	+3	+4	+5
					LOVE						
					MONEY						
					LUCK						
					VITALITY						

23 MONDAY
Moon Age Day 26 • Moon Sign Capricorn

am...

pm...

With a new week in store and not all that much planned, you could find that the start of Monday involves you in comparing, sorting and evolving new ideas. This could prevent much in the way of forward progress but is still an important interlude because it is eventualities that count in the end.

24 TUESDAY
Moon Age Day 27 • Moon Sign Capricorn

am...

pm...

Creative potential seems to be particularly strong at the moment and this would make for an excellent period when it comes to making changes to the decor of your home. Be bold in your dealings with the world at large because you will get much further if others know what to expect of you.

25 WEDNESDAY
Moon Age Day 28 • Moon Sign Aquarius

am...

pm...

Almost from the moment you rise this morning there are signs around that life is going your way. You entertain others without really trying and that makes them work all the harder to please you to. If the day is not exactly exciting, it still turns out to be highly satisfying and full of promise.

26 THURSDAY
Moon Age Day 0 • Moon Sign Aquarius

am...

pm...

Your profile is lower, but that does not mean that you can afford to relax too much. On the whole you may decide that a quieter approach to some situations works better in any case. This is especially true when you are dealing with younger people, some of whom appear to be deliberately awkward.

27 FRIDAY

Moon Age Day 1 • Moon Sign Pisces

am ....

pm ....

It is easy to stand up for yourself but you do have to be a little careful about the sensitivity of those around you. Removing one or two obstacles from your path is part of your planning for today and works well when seen in the longer term. If you are up against some sort of test you should perform well.

28 SATURDAY

Moon Age Day 2 • Moon Sign Pisces

am ....

pm ....

Get any weekend jobs that you have not been looking forward to out of the way as soon as possible, leaving the remainder of the time for pleasing yourself. Some Aries subjects have a definite desire to ring the changes at present and some time spent away from home would suit you fine.

1 SUNDAY

Moon Age Day 3 • Moon Sign Aries

am ....

pm ....

There is little enough time to rest on your laurels today but you probably will not care too much since you are quite anxious to stay out there in the mainstream of life in any case. An entertaining time is at hand, and there are people around who bring a breath of fresh air into your life as the day unfolds.

← NEGATIVE TREND						POSITIVE TREND →				
-5	-4	-3	-2	-1		+1	+2	+3	+4	+5
					LOVE					
					MONEY					
					LUCK					
					VITALITY					

1998

YOUR MONTH AT A GLANCE

The twelve numbered boxes represent the important areas in your life. The key to the numbers you will find beneath the panel. A sun above the number indicates that opportunities are around. A cloud below the number, that you should be a bit defensive. Nothing above or below and life will be pretty ordinary.

1	2	3	4	5	6	7	8	9	10	11	12

KEY

1 Strength of Personality
2 Personal Finance
3 Useful Information Gathering
4 Domestic Affairs
5 Pleasure & Romance
6 Effective Work & Health

7 One to One Relationships
8 Questioning, Thinking & Deciding
9 External Influences / Education
10 Career Aspirations
11 Teamwork Activities
12 Unconscious Impulses

MARCH HIGHS AND LOWS

Here, I show how the rhythm of the Moon will affect you this month. Like the tide, your energies and abilities will rise and fall with its pattern. When it is above the date line, go-for-it. When it is below the line you should be resting.

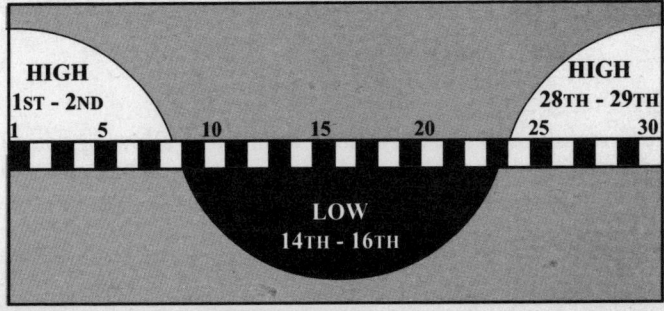

HIGH 1ST - 2ND

HIGH 28TH - 29TH

1   5   10   15   20   25   30

LOW 14TH - 16TH

2 MONDAY
Moon Age Day 4 • Moon Sign Aries

am ....

pm ....

The lunar high is still with you so make sure that you get everything done today that has been outstanding for any length of time. There is no end to your abilities at the moment and you dash through tasks that would normally take you twice the time. A good period to contemplate a professional move.

3 TUESDAY
Moon Age Day 5 • Moon Sign Taurus

am ....

pm ....

Not a time to go it alone. Remember at every turn that there are people around you who are only too willing to share any burden. Part of the problem of being an Aries subject is that you find it difficult to share the less favourable aspects of life with your friends. This is not being entirely fair to you or them.

4 WEDNESDAY
Moon Age Day 6 • Moon Sign Taurus

am ....

pm ....

Not a time to go it alone. Remember at every turn that there are people around you who are only too willing to share any burden. Part of the problem of being an Aries subject is that you find it difficult to share the less favourable aspects of life with your friends. This is not being entirely fair to you or them.

5 THURSDAY
Moon Age Day 7 • Moon Sign Gemini

am ....

pm ....

A boost to social matters comes along at present, allowing you to make the most out of new encounters and an association with people who have not played an important part in your life previously. Once many of the tasks of the day are dealt with you are anxious to get out of the house and enjoy yourself.

6 FRIDAY

Moon Age Day 8 • Moon Sign Gemini

am . . . .

pm . . . .

The spirit is really willing today and that means that your intentions are all fairly honourable too. Of course this does not necessarily come across to those you are dealing with and there is a need to confide your plans if you still want assistance. Routines could get you down, but not if you mix them with pleasant jobs too.

7 SATURDAY

Moon Age Day 9 • Moon Sign Cancer

am . . . .

pm . . . .

Recent energetic trends calm down a little, though this does not prevent you from getting plenty done on this March Saturday. There are domestic responsibilities to think about and you will probably want to spend at least a little time in the company of your relatives, at least one of whom has something to say.

8 SUNDAY

Moon Age Day 10 • Moon Sign Cancer

am . . . .

pm . . . .

The pace of life quickens again and this turns out to be one of the busiest Sundays of the month. It may not be that you have anything much planned, but circumstances take you over and you end up dashing about all the same. Not that this is necessarily a bad thing, as the events of today should prove.

	← *NEGATIVE TREND*						*POSITIVE TREND* →				
	-5	-4	-3	-2	-1		+1	+2	+3	+4	+5
LOVE											
MONEY											
LUCK											
VITALITY											

9 MONDAY
Moon Age Day 11 • Moon Sign Leo

am . . . .

pm . . . .

High spirits are now in evidence and this is an excellent start to the working week for many sons and daughters of Mars. In a professional sense you refuse to put all your eggs in one basket, which turns out to be advantageous. Meanwhile relationships offer you a retreat from the mundane when you need it.

10 TUESDAY
Moon Age Day 12 • Moon Sign Leo

am . . . .

pm . . . .

A red letter day when it comes to social aspects of life, It is not difficult to get on with anyone, even people you have found it difficult to come to terms with in the past. Acting on impulse, you might appear to get yourself into one or two scrapes, but isn't it going to be fun getting yourself out of them again?

11 WEDNESDAY
Moon Age Day 13 • Moon Sign Leo

am . . . .

pm . . . .

You are urged to take the lead as Mars, your ruling planet, becomes especially important in your solar chart. You never turn away from offered responsibility and should be just about equal to any task that you take on for yourself. Only be careful that you do not try to do too much, all at the same time.

12 THURSDAY
Moon Age Day 14 • Moon Sign Virgo

am . . . .

pm . . . .

Still ready for action you could be rather surprised if life slows down around you. This is the sort of situation that you simply have to come to terms with this month, at a time which turns out to be very changeable. Always have a series of less dynamic options open before you and you won't be taken by surprise.

13 FRIDAY
Moon Age Day 15 • Moon Sign Virgo

am...

pm...

Apart from certain specific matters about which you can actually do very little, this is still a period for getting on successfully with life. A few small arguments are likely in the family or amongst friends and although you will not be starting them it does take two to tango. You may be rather happy to be alone.

14 SATURDAY
Moon Age Day 16 • Moon Sign Libra

am...

pm...

The lunar low emphasises the more personal and private elements of your nature right now. If this means that you genuinely do get a well earned rest this will probably be no bad thing. Not everyone seems to behave in a rational way, though it could be your own point of perspective that is slightly distorted.

15 SUNDAY
Moon Age Day 17 • Moon Sign Libra

am...

pm...

Make as much time for rest and relaxation as you are able to do today. This is Sunday after all and you cannot expect to be on the go all the time. What would really suit you is a short trip away from the routines and cares of the domestic scene. Even if this only means a walk it would do you good.

← NEGATIVE TREND							POSITIVE TREND →				
-5	-4	-3	-2	-1			+1	+2	+3	+4	+5
					LOVE						
					MONEY						
					LUCK						
					VITALITY						

16 MONDAY   *Moon Age Day 18 • Moon Sign Libra*

am...

pm...

After a relaxing weekend you are back into the swing of things again and
ready to take on almost anything that the world wants to throw at you.
Much of the day is spent waiting, because there really isn't quite as much
to do as you would wish. That is why, in the end, you become very
inventive.

17 TUESDAY   *Moon Age Day 19 • Moon Sign Scorpio*

am...

pm...

Although there are masses of people around who would be only too
willing to lend a hand, you want to go it alone today. In terms of the way
your mind is working you tend to step back in time, to thoughts and
possibilities that are so private that you could not allow even friends into
the picture.

18 WEDNESDAY   *Moon Age Day 20 • Moon Sign Scorpio*

am...

pm...

You don't need me to tell you that you are a complex character, and that
fact really shows with the level of options open to you now, and the way
that you deal with them. This has to be a key day because so many of the
better possibilities for the future are lighting up the sky of your imagination right now.

19 THURSDAY   *Moon Age Day 21 • Moon Sign Sagittarius*

am...

pm...

Some of the ideas you come up with are quite frankly impractical at the
moment, but that does not mean that they will appear to be so later on.
A good course of action is to forget or cancel nothing. You can put certain
incentives on hold, but you will decide in the end to follow at least one
notion right through.

20 FRIDAY
Moon Age Day 22 • Moon Sign Sagittarius

am ....

pm ....

The Sun enters your solar first house and you stand before a month of good social interaction and a period when you feel rather good about yourself. Although you do not achieve a great deal by rushing you are able to move at lightening speed when it comes to following up in a promising social lead.

21 SATURDAY
Moon Age Day 23 • Moon Sign Sagittarius

am ....

pm ....

The way you manage to turn situations to your own advantage today should have others green with envy. Not that you thinking entirely about yourself because it would be fair to say that you are taking the needs and wants of those around you very much into account. In company your attitude is all important.

22 SUNDAY
Moon Age Day 24 • Moon Sign Capricorn

am ....

pm ....

You are likely to be friendly to everyone today and they will react accordingly. Strangely enough, many of the gains that you make at the moment have not been requested at all, but come along simply because your friends have your best interests at heart. You meet some very kind people at the present time.

← *NEGATIVE TREND*   *POSITIVE TREND* →

-5	-4	-3	-2	-1			+1	+2	+3	+4	+5
					LOVE						
					MONEY						
					LUCK						
					VITALITY						

23 MONDAY   *Moon Age Day 25 • Moon Sign Capricorn*

am ....

pm ....

Whatever you get done today does not have to be tackled tomorrow and
this is the attitude that tends to drive you forward at present. Coming to
terms with situations that troubled you in the past is now a piece of cake,
making today ideal to coax a few skeletons out of the cupboard that is
your past.

24 TUESDAY   *Moon Age Day 26 • Moon Sign Aquarius*

am ....

pm ....

Love matters almost more than anything else today. If you are a single
Aries subject you will be making the most out of this fact by coming to
terms with possible new relationships. For more settled children of Mars
there is the promise of a happy spell when you are in the company of
really special individuals.

25 WEDNESDAY   *Moon Age Day 27 • Moon Sign Aquarius*

am ....

pm ....

You cannot live your life through the ideas or motivations of others, a fact
that you tend to realise instinctively. It's a pity that other people do not
feel the same way and it is possible that you will have to make them
aware of the fact. An occasional obstacle comes along now but you deal
with them as and when you must.

26 THURSDAY   *Moon Age Day 28 • Moon Sign Pisces*

am ....

pm ....

Forget about the cares of the mundane world for an hour or two and
concentrate instead on having a really good time. Sporting Aries subjects
can get a great deal from today and will be making the most of any
opportunity that comes along. Fresh air suits you all right now and you
cannot get enough of it.

27 FRIDAY
Moon Age Day 29 • Moon Sign Pisces

am . . . .

pm . . . .

The present position of the Sun in your chart is a cause of quite definite inspiration today, because you are getting on nearly as well with yourself as you are able to do with others. The slightly quiet trends that reside at the back of your mind mean having to be pensive on occasions, though not for long.

28 SATURDAY ♦
Moon Age Day 0 • Moon Sign Aries

am . . . .

pm . . . .

Lunar high time follows up on the very positive trends that began to show themselves yesterday. This is the time of the month to make a big pile of all your plans and to start going for gold with all of them. Life helps you out when you need it to do so the most and you tend to be very optimistic.

29 SUNDAY ♦
Moon Age Day 1 • Moon Sign Aries

am . . . .

pm . . . .

Kind and considerate, you do whatever you can to help people on the way now. The funny thing is that most of them also appear to be in just the right position to do you a favour too. Practical matters are a piece of cake to deal with and this is the best day for some time to take a chance or two.

← NEGATIVE TREND						POSITIVE TREND →				
-5	-4	-3	-2	-1		+1	+2	+3	+4	+5
					LOVE	▓	▓			
					MONEY	▓	▓			
					LUCK	▓				
					VITALITY	▓				

30 MONDAY ♦ *Moon Age Day 2 • Moon Sign Taurus*

am ....

pm ....

Details are something of a bind at the start of the new working week, but these should not hold you back for very long. Not everyone seems to have your best interests at heart but that won't hold you back very much either. Progress is not quite so evident today, but it is possible all the same.

31 TUESDAY ♦ *Moon Age Day 3 • Moon Sign Taurus*

am ....

pm ....

Minor financial gains seem likely at the moment, even if the sort of risk-taking exercise of a couple of days ago is not to be recommended. It is most probable that whatever advantages do come your way can be directly traced to the positive way you have been dealing with friends and associates alike.

1 WEDNESDAY ♦ *Moon Age Day 4 • Moon Sign Gemini*

am ....

pm ....

Today may seem like climbing a hill that has no real summit. Now let us get this straight. If you really want to pit your wits against the whole world, and for no good reason, nobody is going to be in a position to prevent you from doing so. In the end the decisions is yours, and you could opt for solitude instead.

2 THURSDAY ♦ *Moon Age Day 5 • Moon Sign Gemini*

am ....

pm ....

Travel of any sort really suits you now and there is a tendency to feel restless if you are confined in any way and unable to bring the breeze of new experience into your life. Start as you mean to go on, so that even if it is not possible to make a journey for today, you are at least planning one for later.

3 FRIDAY ♦ *Moon Age Day 6 • Moon Sign Cancer*

am . . . .

pm . . . .

As you seem to be more interested in personal ambitions right now, most of your energy seems to be put into new professional ventures of one sort or another. On the way leave just a little time free for being with family and friends, all of whom have been missing your special attention for a few days.

4 SATURDAY ♦ *Moon Age Day 7 • Moon Sign Cancer*

am . . . .

pm . . . .

You are quire frankly in a class of your own today and happy to be in the limelight that present planetary trends provide. It may seem as though you can have almost anything you want, as long as you remember that there is invariably a price to be paid. When you have made up your mind, stand by your opinions.

5 SUNDAY ♦ *Moon Age Day 8 • Moon Sign Cancer*

am . . . .

pm . . . .

Actions speak louder than words in your life and today proves to be no exception with that regard. People really do want to listen to what you have to say though, so it is important to take time out to talk. Sunday means at least some time for pleasing yourself, and the evening may turn out to be the best chance.

← NEGATIVE TREND						POSITIVE TREND →				
-5	-4	-3	-2	-1		+1	+2	+3	+4	+5
					LOVE					
					MONEY					
					LUCK					
					VITALITY					

1998

YOUR MONTH AT A GLANCE

The twelve numbered boxes represent the important areas in your life. The key to the numbers you will find beneath the panel. A sun above the number indicates that opportunities are around. A cloud below the number, that you should be a bit defensive. Nothing above or below and life will be pretty ordinary.

1	2	3	4	5	6	7	8	9	10	11	12

KEY

1 Strength of Personality
2 Personal Finance
3 Useful Information Gathering
4 Domestic Affairs
5 Pleasure & Romance
6 Effective Work & Health

7 One to One Relationships
8 Questioning, Thinking & Deciding
9 External Influences / Education
10 Career Aspirations
11 Teamwork Activities
12 Unconscious Impulses

APRIL HIGHS AND LOWS

Here, I show how the rhythm of the Moon will affect you this month. Like the tide, your energies and abilities will rise and fall with its pattern. When it is above the date line, go-for-it. When it is below the line you should be resting.

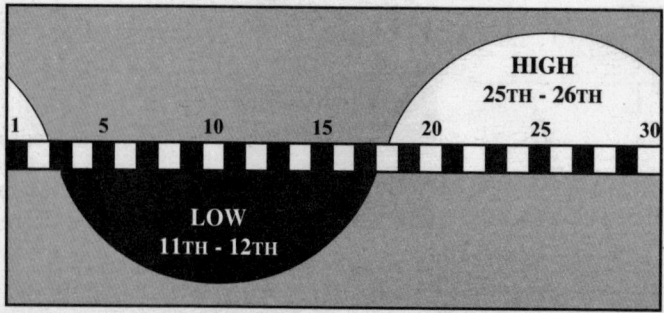

HIGH
25TH - 26TH

1   5   10   15   20   25   30

LOW
11TH - 12TH

6 MONDAY   ♦   *Moon Age Day 9 • Moon Sign Leo*

am . . . .

pm . . . .

Relationships stand out as being the most important aspect of your life today and you will be doing everything that you can to pep them up in one way or another. The way friends are behaving could mystify you a little and you will need to do a little delving to find out what the problem might be.

7 TUESDAY   ♦   *Moon Age Day 10 • Moon Sign Leo*

am . . . .

pm . . . .

Although the practical necessities of life can cause you a little concern early in the day, it is not likely that such considerations will remain with you much beyond the middle of the morning. For one thing you are too busy to be worried for very long, and you also find that answers come from surprising directions.

8 WEDNESDAY   ♦   *Moon Age Day 11 • Moon Sign Virgo*

am . . . .

pm . . . .

Catch up on your need to organise yourself more. This is a good time for getting the facts and figures together to make progress in a financial matter that could have been concerning you for a while. Out of the ordinary experiences are still likely and your intuition seems to be honed to perfection.

9 THURSDAY   ♦   *Moon Age Day 12 • Moon Sign Virgo*

am . . . .

pm . . . .

Others may think differently to you at present, but that is no reason for simply abandoning your own considerations and going with the flow. On the contrary, if you know that you are right, even in the face of a whole world that says the reverse is true. you should still carry and on and do your own thing.

10 FRIDAY ♦ *Moon Age Day 13 • Moon Sign Virgo*

am..

pm..

The lunar low holds you back a little, or at least that is how it seems at present. The truth is probably very much different because all that is really happening is that you are being forced to take careful stock of situations. Since being impetuous is sometimes a problem to you, the present trends could be helpful.

11 SATURDAY ♦ *Moon Age Day 14 • Moon Sign Libra*

am..

pm..

Spirits may not be exactly high, and yet as long as you are willing to wait just a day or so, prospects look extremely good. This period is ideal for talking matters through with someone you love very much and for making progress of a personal nature with those who have been rather withdrawn recently.

12 SUNDAY ♦ *Moon Age Day 15 • Moon Sign Libra*

am..

pm..

Matters that you have had to put to the back of your mind become very topical again today. Acting on impulse becomes possible later in the day, and continues through much of the coming week. There ought to be plenty of compliments coming your way at the present time and you do plenty to cheer friends up.

← NEGATIVE TREND							POSITIVE TREND →			
-5	-4	-3	-2	-1			+1	+2	+3	+4	+5
					LOVE						
					MONEY						
					LUCK						
					VITALITY						

13 MONDAY ♦ *Moon Age Day 16 • Moon Sign Scorpio*

am ....

pm ....

A careful search may be necessary if you want to put your hand on something that you have mislaid. Enlist the support of others, one or two of whom may have a better idea where to look than you have. It is possible that you will discover something of great importance whilst you are sifting through things.

14 TUESDAY ♦ *Moon Age Day 17 • Moon Sign Scorpio*

am ....

pm ....

You appear to wander through life without a care in the world now. The natural sunshine that is always shining deep down inside you now finds its way to the surface and you have a wealth of interesting facts and figures at the tips of your fingers. More important than any other fact, you are particularly cheerful.

15 WEDNESDAY ♦ *Moon Age Day 18 • Moon Sign Scorpio*

am ....

pm ....

You have worked long and hard to achieve a particular objective and you are not at all willing to let go of it now, simply because someone you know well does not agree with you. What is needed right now is an injection of self-belief, together with the realisation that your own efforts count more than anything.

16 THURSDAY ♦ *Moon Age Day 19 • Moon Sign Sagittarius*

am ....

pm ....

There is no point at all in believing everything you hear, if only because a proportion of it cannot be true. Follow your own convictions today and you really cannot go far wrong. Nobody has the monopoly on wisdom, least of all you, but there is a chance that you are displaying common sense today.

17 FRIDAY ◆ *Moon Age Day 20 • Moon Sign Sagittarius*

am ....

pm ....

Get out and about as much as you can since this is not a day to be tied down to convention or trapped in situations that you find you be distinctly tedious. Light filters into the darkness of a situation that has been very difficult to sort out in the past. This might be as a result of some timely advice from friends.

18 SATURDAY ◆ *Moon Age Day 21 • Moon Sign Capricorn*

am ....

pm ....

Although the weekend is here it is towards the professional aspects of life that you turn much of your attention at the moment. Now you realise that you are starting to achieve a personal peak of action and determination. Whatever you turn your hand to at present, you can expect to succeed.

19 SUNDAY ◆ *Moon Age Day 22 • Moon Sign Capricorn*

am ....

pm ....

Curb spendthrift tendencies as much as you can because although there is probably enough money to go around at present, it is likely that you will not consider yourself to be wealthy. There are very much better times ahead and it only really takes a steady hand on the financial tiller to see you through.

← NEGATIVE TREND							POSITIVE TREND →				
-5	-4	-3	-2	-1			+1	+2	+3	+4	+5
					LOVE						
					MONEY						
					LUCK						
					VITALITY						

20 MONDAY   *Moon Age Day 23 • Moon Sign Aquarius*

am ....

pm ....

The Sun moves into your solar second house and brings with it a month long period when you feel the stability of your past planning on the material front. For the first time in ages this means that you can follow up on a host of possibilities that have had to remain on the back burner for quite a long time.

21 TUESDAY   *Moon Age Day 24 • Moon Sign Aquarius*

am ....

pm ....

Is it really that others are especially difficult to deal with or have you simply got yourself into a strange frame of mind that makes the world look odd? The truth is probably somewhere between the two, which is why you find yourself spending a proportion of today thinking things through and talking to friends.

22 WEDNESDAY   *Moon Age Day 25 • Moon Sign Aquarius*

am ....

pm ....

Pouring masses of energy into those directions that are already working well for you is not to be recommended at the moment. It is important for Aries subjects to learn when they should tamper with things, and when to leave well enough alone. Life generally is more successful than you think now.

23 THURSDAY   *Moon Age Day 26 • Moon Sign Pisces*

am ....

pm ....

Home and family are very important factors in your life ahead of the lunar high. Spend some time communicating with your nearest and dearest, which is not the same thing as talking at them. You can expect gains to be forthcoming and should feel the power of love working steadily in your life.

24 FRIDAY

Moon Age Day 27 • Moon Sign Pisces

am . . . .

pm . . . .

An atmospheric period, when it is possible to see things that are genuinely beyond the scope of your comprehension as a rule. Even fairly distant friends manage to be of great help to you at present, whilst colleagues may be thinking up ways that your professional desires can be realised in the weeks ahead.

25 SATURDAY

Moon Age Day 28 • Moon Sign Aries

am . . . .

pm . . . .

An tendency to feel tired this weekend is now out of the window once and for all. Although the pressures of life might have made themselves known at various stages during the last month, they have no power to hold you back now. An interesting interlude is brought about courtesy of the lunar high.

26 SUNDAY

Moon Age Day 0 • Moon Sign Aries

am . . . .

pm . . . .

Good luck attends most of your efforts today and you are able to get yourself into gear ahead of a week that you correctly suspect is going to be of supreme importance. Give the best of yourself to life and to others and you really cannot go far wrong. Personally speaking the world should be your oyster today.

← *NEGATIVE TREND*						*POSITIVE TREND* →				
-5	-4	-3	-2	-1		+1	+2	+3	+4	+5
					LOVE					
					MONEY					
					LUCK					
					VITALITY					

27 MONDAY   *Moon Age Day 1 • Moon Sign Taurus*

am...

pm...

You may find that you are disregarding the opinions of others if they do not conform to what you believe yourself. This is a fact of life that many Aries subjects must come to terms with at one time or another and your present 'certainty' about anything and everything may have to be suppressed a little.

28 TUESDAY   *Moon Age Day 2 • Moon Sign Taurus*

am...

pm...

Life is still working on your side, even if you have to calm yourself down in the face of some fairly exciting possibilities. Take all your fences one at a time and it looks as though you are heading for a clear round. Vitality may be higher than you have been expecting and optimism is also present.

29 WEDNESDAY   *Moon Age Day 3 • Moon Sign Gemini*

am...

pm...

Keep your mind on the task in hand, at least whilst the working day lasts. Later on you can afford to please yourself a little more and will take delight is doing whatever you really wish in a personal and social sense. Friends have it in mind to support you if they feel you are being used or taken for granted.

30 THURSDAY   *Moon Age Day 4 • Moon Sign Gemini*

am...

pm...

There are some very receptive types about, so there has rarely been a better time for speaking your mind. Of course you will do so in a tactful and considerate way and should be willing to see the point of view that others are putting forward. It takes time to plan a journey for the future, but keep plugging away.

1 FRIDAY

Moon Age Day 5 • Moon Sign Cancer

am ....

pm ....

The tempo of day to day affairs is quickened significantly at the end of this working week and so you probably find yourself living through a Friday that passes in a flash. A particular task in life that you have really been enjoying needs to be finished off now, so that you can clear the decks for new projects.

2 SATURDAY

Moon Age Day 6 • Moon Sign Cancer

am ....

pm ....

It's hard to see how others could consider you to be selfish, simply because you know that you are right about something at present. The fact is that they will not do so, just as long as you take the time out to keep them informed, whilst not changing your mind once it is made up. A balancing act is called for.

3 SUNDAY

Moon Age Day 7 • Moon Sign Leo

am ....

pm ....

Venus enters your solar first house, which is bound to bring a boost to personal relationships and the way that you choose to view them. Beyond your own control however is the rise of popularity that comes about. Someone you have admired for a long time now has some fascinating things to say about you.

← NEGATIVE TREND							POSITIVE TREND →				
-5	-4	-3	-2	-1			+1	+2	+3	+4	+5
					LOVE						
					MONEY						
					LUCK						
					VITALITY						

106

1998

YOUR MONTH AT A GLANCE

The twelve numbered boxes represent the important areas in your life. The key to the numbers you will find beneath the panel. A sun above the number indicates that opportunities are around. A cloud below the number, that you should be a bit defensive. Nothing above or below and life will be pretty ordinary.

1	2	3	4	5	6	7	8	9	10	11	12

(Sun symbols above numbers 3, 9 and 11. Cloud symbols below numbers 1 and 5.)

KEY

1 Strength of Personality
2 Personal Finance
3 Useful Information Gathering
4 Domestic Affairs
5 Pleasure & Romance
6 Effective Work & Health

7 One to One Relationships
8 Questioning, Thinking & Deciding
9 External Influences / Education
10 Career Aspirations
11 Teamwork Activities
12 Unconscious Impulses

MAY HIGHS AND LOWS

Here, I show how the rhythm of the Moon will affect you this month. Like the tide, your energies and abilities will rise and fall with its pattern. When it is above the date line, go-for-it. When it is below the line you should be resting.

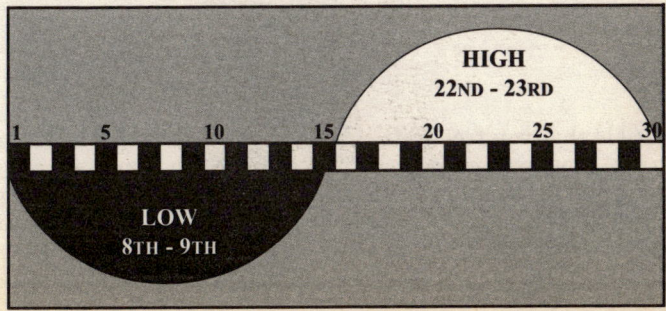

HIGH
22ND – 23RD

LOW
8TH – 9TH

4 MONDAY

Moon Age Day 8 • Moon Sign Leo

am ....

pm ....

The keenest of people crop up at the start of this week and most of them have the same sort of incentives that appeal to you too. Any sort of research is valid today, as long as it pushes you further down the road towards your chosen objectives. There is not much likelihood of boredom on what should be a busy day.

5 TUESDAY

Moon Age Day 9 • Moon Sign Virgo

am ....

pm ....

Once you get a specific idea into your head it is unlikely that you would let go of it again in a hurry. This can be a good thing but it really depends on what path you are choosing to follow. Don't be too quick to jump to the assistance of a colleague unless you know exactly what they are doing.

6 WEDNESDAY

Moon Age Day 10 • Moon Sign Virgo

am ....

pm ....

There are certain tasks that you simply have to get out of the way today before you can begin to enjoy yourself in the way that you really wish to. Look out for a little assistance from family members and possibly also from friends but realise that not everyone around you at present is on the same wavelength.

7 THURSDAY

Moon Age Day 11 • Moon Sign Virgo

am ....

pm ....

It is possible that you feel a little down in the mouth this morning and with no real good reason that you know about. Such trends are not going to last long and the best course of action may well be to work through the phase. By the afternoon you should be firing on all cylinders again.

8 FRIDAY
Moon Age Day 12 • Moon Sign Libra

am . . . .

pm . . . .

Keep your eye on the ball today and don't allow yourself to be distracted by details that have nothing at all to do with you personally. Gains come along regarding your social life and this is not the time to turn down any reasonable suggestion for getting out and about in the company of faithful and enduring friends.

9 SATURDAY
Moon Age Day 13 • Moon Sign Libra

am . . . .

pm . . . .

It might be best to allow your partner, or perhaps a family member, to do something on your behalf at the moment. There are one or two aspects of life that you are not seeing quite as clearly as would normally be the case and you could do with an hour or two to simply sit and think before today is over.

10 SUNDAY
Moon Age Day 14 • Moon Sign Scorpio

am . . . .

pm . . . .

Family finances could be on your mind today and it would be worthwhile having a discussion with family members before you make up your mind to take any particular action regarding them. Meanwhile there is ever possibility that romance will be entering your life in a way you did not expect.

← *NEGATIVE TREND*   *POSITIVE TREND* →

-5	-4	-3	-2	-1		+1	+2	+3	+4	+5
					LOVE					
					MONEY					
					LUCK					
					VITALITY					

11 MONDAY
Moon Age Day 15 • Moon Sign Scorpio

am...

pm...

If you take a liberty or two today you can at least be fairly certain that you will get away with doing so. The real cheek of Aries shows itself at this time and there is very little that you would fail to get from others if you are willing to put your mind to the task. Keep an eye on younger family members.

12 TUESDAY
Moon Age Day 16 • Moon Sign Scorpio

am...

pm...

Although today justifiably carries the key day symbol, it is behind closed doors that the very best trends are going to show themselves. It may not be possible to make much in the way of professional progress at the moment, though in many ways you do not really care whilst you are so happy personally speaking.

13 WEDNESDAY
Moon Age Day 17 • Moon Sign Sagittarius

am...

pm...

The chance to broaden your horizons in one way or another is something that you will not turn down at this stage of the month. Your eyes are wide open and you seem to be less inclined to stay at home than was the case yesterday. Finalising plans for a journey to be taken later is important at some stage.

14 THURSDAY
Moon Age Day 18 • Moon Sign Sagittarius

am...

pm...

Although you feel rather more lazy than would usually be the case for the sign of Aries, this may not turn out to be a bad situation at all. For one thing there are people around who want to do you favours and some of them may know what is best and most comfortable for you now. Go along with the happy flow.

15 FRIDAY
Moon Age Day 19 • Moon Sign Capricorn

am . . . .

pm . . . .

This is definitely the right time to try out the sort of new ideas that involve dipping a toe into the water of life, not jumping in altogether. A fairly entertaining interlude seems to be on the cards, even if you would find it difficult to get your way quite to the extent to which you would like to become accustomed.

16 SATURDAY
Moon Age Day 20 • Moon Sign Capricorn

am . . . .

pm . . . .

After a somewhat less positive spell concerning your professional life, Saturday could well bring a fair share of new ideas that can be put into practice next week. As a result you could spend a little time thinking about matters. On the other hand your social impulses are also strong and worth chasing.

17 SUNDAY
Moon Age Day 21 • Moon Sign Capricorn

am . . . .

pm . . . .

Anything that you are doing alongside other people should prove to be more than worthwhile today. There are times when you forget how to relax and the beauty of a day such as this one is that you learn about yourself through the observation of those around you. At the very least a truly contented sort of day.

← *NEGATIVE TREND*								*POSITIVE TREND* →				
-5	-4	-3	-2	-1			+1	+2	+3	+4	+5
					LOVE						
					MONEY						
					LUCK						
					VITALITY						

18 MONDAY   *Moon Age Day 22 • Moon Sign Aquarius*

am ....

pm ....

Your powers of attraction appear to know no bounds at present and you can easily come to terms with someone who has probably been important to you for some time. Not everyone is susceptible to your charm at first, though present trends being what they are, you should soon bring them round.

19 TUESDAY   *Moon Age Day 23 • Moon Sign Aquarius*

am ....

pm ....

Let the world pass you by for a few hours if that is what it wishes to do on this particular Tuesday. With drive and determination put away in the garage for a few hours you should be content to drift on the tide of life and would not be worried about losing headway. Tomorrow is another and a different day.

20 WEDNESDAY   *Moon Age Day 24 • Moon Sign Pisces*

am ....

pm ....

It is money that you tend to look at now, the more so because it may seem as though those in your immediate vicinity are failing to address this most important commodity. Do you think you may be taking yourself and life a little too seriously? Fortunately you are never far from a laugh at any stage today.

21 THURSDAY   *Moon Age Day 25 • Moon Sign Pisces*

am ....

pm ....

There is double the reason to celebrate today since the lunar high is approaching, whilst the Sun also enters your solar third house. Translated this means your communication skills are excellent and that you can turn the fact into positive good luck. Money matters are less important, yet more settled.

22 FRIDAY   *Moon Age Day 26 • Moon Sign Aries*

am . . . .

pm . . . .

The Moon offers you an Aladdin's Cave of possibilities at the end of this
working week. Most important of all is the chance to take all your
carefully selected plans and put them into action. What cannot be
achieved ahead of the weekend must wait because you need the time to
enjoy yourself too at some stage.

23 SATURDAY   *Moon Age Day 27 • Moon Sign Aries*

am . . . .

pm . . . .

Part of a three day festival of fun, you cannot take the events of this
Saturday all that seriously. There are many laughs for the taking and a
good many genuinely funny people around. It seems as though having a
good time is the most important ingredient today and that involves being
with your friends.

24 SUNDAY   *Moon Age Day 28 • Moon Sign Taurus*

am . . . .

pm . . . .

The Moon moves on and today could feel a little lack lustre after the more
open and dynamic trends of the last few days. You are more willing to
centre your attention on more mundane matters and should also find
that a great many routines can be played out, though without boring
yourself on the way.

← *NEGATIVE TREND*						*POSITIVE TREND* →				
-5	-4	-3	-2	-1		+1	+2	+3	+4	+5
					LOVE					
					MONEY					
					LUCK					
					VITALITY					

25 MONDAY   *Moon Age Day 0 • Moon Sign Taurus*

am . . . .

pm . . . .

Just the right day to protect your financial interests, though how you go about doing so depends upon individual circumstances and takes a combination of common sense and intuition. It's hard to imagine that you could become bored at present since you have so very much to do with yourself.

26 TUESDAY   *Moon Age Day 1 • Moon Sign Gemini*

am . . . .

pm . . . .

An important matter is settled with a little of the ingenuity which started to show itself in you during the last couple of days. You have a very light and yet positive touch on the buttons of life at present and need to be certain that your hunches are going to pay off. Friends tend to trust you quite willingly at present.

27 WEDNESDAY   *Moon Age Day 2 • Moon Sign Gemini*

am . . . .

pm . . . .

You may encounter a little opposition today and there is really nothing that you can do about the situation apart from being aware that it exists and making up your mind not to allow it to get in the way. Criticism is like water off a duck's back in any case right now and you will only do exactly what you want in the end.

28 THURSDAY   *Moon Age Day 3 • Moon Sign Cancer*

am . . . .

pm . . . .

It looks as though you are now looking for the best of both worlds, since you want to stay out there in the mainstream of life and yet find relationships to be of supreme importance. As long as you remember that most important of words, 'balance', there should be no problem at all. An unexpected journey is possible.

29 FRIDAY
Moon Age Day 4 • Moon Sign Cancer

am . . . .

pm . . . .

Someone has a wealth of good ideas of their own at present, but since these may have a bearing on your life too it would be worth listening to what they have to say. In general terms this is an up and down sort of day but it is the essence of the Aries subject to be able to take the rough with the smooth.

30 SATURDAY
Moon Age Day 5 • Moon Sign Cancer

am . . . .

pm . . . .

Venus is strong for you and there is every possibility that life works its magic in terms of your personal life today. If you are a single Aries who has been looking for love, you should not have to cast your gaze much further. For most children of Aries this is a day to enjoy personal attachments of all kinds.

31 SUNDAY
Moon Age Day 6 • Moon Sign Leo

am . . . .

pm . . . .

Socially speaking this should turn out to be a fun day and it is fortunate for many of you that such trends have come along on a Saturday. You can have a great deal of what you want from life right now and there probably will not be the same sort of price to pay that appears to have been the case for some weeks.

← NEGATIVE TREND								POSITIVE TREND →				
-5	-4	-3	-2	-1			+1	+2	+3	+4	+5
					LOVE						
					MONEY						
					LUCK						
					VITALITY						

1998

YOUR MONTH AT A GLANCE

The twelve numbered boxes represent the important areas in your life. The key to the numbers you will find beneath the panel. A sun above the number indicates that opportunities are around. A cloud below the number, that you should be a bit defensive. Nothing above or below and life will be pretty ordinary.

| 1 | 2 | 3 | 4 | 5 | 6 | 7 | 8 | 9 | 10 | 11 | 12 |

Sun above: 1, 6, 8. Cloud below: 4, 10.

KEY

1 Strength of Personality
2 Personal Finance
3 Useful Information Gathering
4 Domestic Affairs
5 Pleasure & Romance
6 Effective Work & Health

7 One to One Relationships
8 Questioning, Thinking & Deciding
9 External Influences / Education
10 Career Aspirations
11 Teamwork Activities
12 Unconscious Impulses

JUNE HIGHS AND LOWS

Here, I show how the rhythm of the Moon will affect you this month. Like the tide, your energies and abilities will rise and fall with its pattern. When it is above the date line, go-for-it. When it is below the line you should be resting.

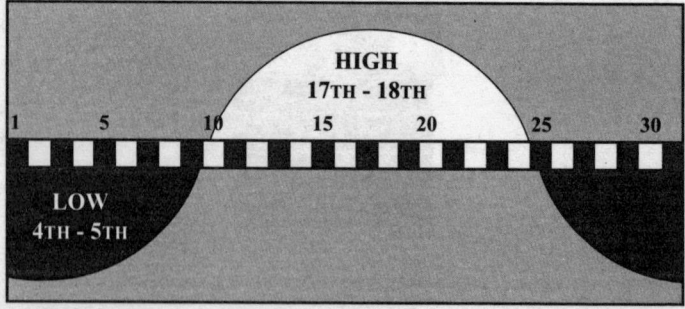

HIGH
17TH - 18TH

LOW
4TH - 5TH

1 MONDAY   *Moon Age Day 7 • Moon Sign Leo*

am ....

pm ....

A good morning for information gathering, followed by an afternoon when you are likely to put what you have learned to the test. Someone comes knocking on your door with a request that you should find intriguing and impossible to refuse. Be fairly bold when it comes to getting your message across.

2 TUESDAY   *Moon Age Day 8 • Moon Sign Virgo*

am ....

pm ....

Try not to be so much of a perfectionist. Half way to achieving all you want today will probably be quite enough and in any case you expect more of yourself than anyone else does. In a personal sense you tend to be much more reasonable and can make significant gains from one-to-one attachments.

3 WEDNESDAY   *Moon Age Day 9 • Moon Sign Virgo*

am ....

pm ....

The good things in life tend to come looking for you, which will make a change after a period when it has been necessary for you to go out and look for them. Not that the change in circumstances is really going to alter many aspects of your life because you are incapable of inactivity at present.

4 THURSDAY   *Moon Age Day 10 • Moon Sign Libra*

am ....

pm ....

With the lunar low comes a slight reversal of some of the more favourable trends that have been with you during the last week or so. Now you really can afford to take things a little more steadily because you won't get anywhere at all by rushing fences that probably don't even exist.

5 FRIDAY

Moon Age Day 11 • Moon Sign Libra

am ....

pm ....

Things are still not exactly exciting in your life as a whole, though you will have time to do some thinking and to collect a few notions together that you can turn to your advantage when the prospects are a little more exciting. Not that you end the working week on a bad note, simply a quiet one.

6 SATURDAY

Moon Age Day 12 • Moon Sign Scorpio

am ....

pm ....

Although you may be rather more emotional than usual this turns out to be an aspect that works to your advantage since it proves your humanity to those around you. Not that you would be looking for pity because you are fully in charge of most situations and even view relationships with optimism.

7 SUNDAY

Moon Age Day 13 • Moon Sign Scorpio

am ....

pm ....

Things get hectic again, which could be rather a shame on a Sunday when everyone around you seems happy to take a stroll in the garden or a trip into the country. Keep the intense activity inside your head and you too can make the most of a June Sunday. Store up real energy until tomorrow.

← NEGATIVE TREND							POSITIVE TREND →			
-5	-4	-3	-2	-1		+1	+2	+3	+4	+5
					LOVE					
					MONEY					
					LUCK					
					VITALITY					

8 MONDAY   *Moon Age Day 14 • Moon Sign Sagittarius*

am . . . .

pm . . . .

Material considerations are on your mind today and you decide that this is the right time for pushing forward, particularly on the work front. A refusal to discuss some matter or other about which you have a singular attitude will not help and the best of the day means some genuine co-operation.

9 TUESDAY   *Moon Age Day 15 • Moon Sign Sagittarius*

am . . . .

pm . . . .

Two minds are quite often better than one, as you will find today if you are willing to listen to what your friends have to say. There really are some excellent ideas about at present and you need the cut and thrust that comes from interaction. Routines do not have the power to get you down - you ignore them!

10 WEDNESDAY   *Moon Age Day 16 • Moon Sign Sagittarius*

am . . . .

pm . . . .

Your powers of positive discrimination are especially useful at the moment and you know in an instant what will work and what cannot. An adventurous phase is at hand and you have all the necessary components to make this into a quite special sort of day. Some personal frustrations are possible however.

11 THURSDAY   *Moon Age Day 17 • Moon Sign Capricorn*

am . . . .

pm . . . .

Professional matters are less than smooth right now, mainly thanks to a particular person who has the tremendous knack of throwing a spanner in the works. All you can do at the end of the day is to laugh at situations that you cannot control. Finances should be strengthening before very long.

12 FRIDAY
Moon Age Day 18 • Moon Sign Capricorn

am . . . .

pm . . . .

Keeping up a high profile and showing your personality to the world you give all you can to projects that have a distinct and unusual appeal. The ordinary is not really of much interest to you at the moment and you set off on a journey of discovery around your own unusual and very original mind.

13 SATURDAY
Moon Age Day 19 • Moon Sign Aquarius

am . . . .

pm . . . .

Your mind is probably filled with the knowledge of all that you have to do, so much so that you might fail to see the wood for the trees. Try to slow things down just a little and approach situations one at the time. This is sound advice, but of the sort that Aries people find difficult to take.

14 SUNDAY
Moon Age Day 20 • Moon Sign Aquarius

am . . . .

pm . . . .

Some unsuspected help comes along today and probably at just the right time too. Any little frustrations early in the day are less than likely to hold you back later on and you manage to split the day between practical requirements and personal choices. Probably a good time for a spring clean at home.

← NEGATIVE TREND						POSITIVE TREND →				
-5	-4	-3	-2	-1		+1	+2	+3	+4	+5
					LOVE					
					MONEY					
					LUCK					
					VITALITY					

15 MONDAY
Moon Age Day 21 • Moon Sign Pisces

am ....

pm ....

There is a lively atmosphere gathering around you at the start of this working week, so much so that you do all you can to milk it. Does this mean being selfish? Probably, but since you are more than willing to put yourself out for others too there is little chance that you run foul of anyone's good will.

16 TUESDAY
Moon Age Day 22 • Moon Sign Pisces

am ....

pm ....

Some unexpected and willing assistance once again shows itself. There is no shortage of help at any stage this month, even if you sometimes have to look for it. This certainly is not the case today and you will be surrounded by offers, some of which you simply cannot accept. Your sensitivity is especially high.

17 WEDNESDAY
Moon Age Day 23 • Moon Sign Aries

am ....

pm ....

The middle of the week brings the lunar high, and probably the most productive phase of the month so far. Get yourself into gear early in the day and make certain that you try out a new incentive or two at this most helpful of times. Money matters are clearly on your mind and you should feel yourself better off.

18 THURSDAY
Moon Age Day 24 • Moon Sign Aries

am ....

pm ....

Some extraordinary possibilities surround you at this time and you will not want to miss a second of all the exciting prospects that are now in store. A good time to make a journey or for moving house. Where circumstances predict you must stay put you will still be forcing changes through.

19 FRIDAY
Moon Age Day 25 • Moon Sign Taurus

am . . . .

pm . . . .
Some luck is still with you, though it might be sensible to avoid pushing it too far today. Chances are that you will be looking for a slightly quieter day because you need to sort out the details of all the schemes and ideas that have been bombarding you of late. End the working week with a sort out.

20 SATURDAY
Moon Age Day 26 • Moon Sign Taurus

am . . . .

pm . . . .
Even the most minor eventuality, if followed through to its logical conclusion, can have the most tremendous part to play in pushing you forward. This is a fact that you tend to realise instinctively today. Meanwhile you could feel in the mood for a shopping spree, possibly alongside some dear friends.

21 SUNDAY
Moon Age Day 27 • Moon Sign Gemini

am . . . .

pm . . . .
The Sun now enters your solar fourth house, bringing with it a month or so when all matters domestic take up a good deal of your thinking and actions. There is no real rush today and you should make the most of any good weather that might be about in order to simply please yourself. Good fortune beckons.

← NEGATIVE TREND						POSITIVE TREND →				
-5	-4	-3	-2	-1		+1	+2	+3	+4	+5
					LOVE					
					MONEY					
					LUCK					
					VITALITY					

22 MONDAY   *Moon Age Day 28 • Moon Sign Gemini*

am ....

pm ....

Although your mind is clearly on the go from the very start of today, it could take your body just a little while to catch up. Be fair on yourself because you often push yourself far harder than is either wise or necessary. At the very least restrict yourself to doing no more than ten or twelve jobs at the same time.

23 TUESDAY   *Moon Age Day 29 • Moon Sign Cancer*

am ....

pm ....

A particular friendship should leave you in no doubt at the moment as to the strength of affections that surround you. It is possible that you will be quite touched by the way those around you react and you can expect yourself to act positively on their behalf in return. Contentment is likely.

24 WEDNESDAY   *Moon Age Day 30 • Moon Sign Cancer*

am ....

pm ....

You certainly have the knack of bringing out the best in others, and never more so than today. This might be associated with a particularly close relationship but is equally likely to strike home in terms of a routine friendship. Wherever it comes from, your attachment is happy and very profitable.

25 THURSDAY   *Moon Age Day 1 • Moon Sign Cancer*

am ....

pm ....

Although a number of your plans at the moment lack substance, they are worth looking at carefully all the same. A bond of genuine affection still exists between yourself and a number of other people. This is positive of course, but has been known to get in the way of true Arian single-minded progress.

26 FRIDAY
Moon Age Day 2 • Moon Sign Leo

am ....

pm ....

The influences of today certainly bring out the best in you. It would be almost impossible to avoid being altruistic and helpful this month, as you have already discovered, so there is not much point in trying. You may not be ready for sainthood just yet but you care deeply about your friends and colleagues.

27 SATURDAY
Moon Age Day 3 • Moon Sign Leo

am ....

pm ....

Ensure that you leave plenty of time for simply pleasing yourself. June has meant a whole succession of weekends that have fallen at times when trends favoured relaxation. This weekend is no exception. Entertainment is not hard to find, and comes from family, friends and even strangers.

28 SUNDAY
Moon Age Day 4 • Moon Sign Virgo

am ....

pm ....

Would you believe it? There is even time today to spend in hobbies or other activities that have no relevance to your life in a material or practical sense whatsoever. Of course this does not matter at all, just as long as you are having a good time. Create space for some day-dreams, which are also important.

← NEGATIVE TREND							POSITIVE TREND →			
-5	-4	-3	-2	-1		+1	+2	+3	+4	+5
					LOVE					
					MONEY					
					LUCK					
					VITALITY					

29 MONDAY   *Moon Age Day 5 • Moon Sign Virgo*

am ....

pm ....

Personal and private matters are something that you would wish to keep that way, not that you are likely to get the chance right now. The simple truth is that others are interested to know what makes you tick and will be particularly nosy in their way of finding out. Don't get frustrated by the fact.

30 TUESDAY   *Moon Age Day 6 • Moon Sign Virgo*

am ....

pm ....

A new but brief phase encourages you to look to your social life, more in the way that an Air sign type of individual may do. In some ways this makes you appear to be a stranger when you are viewed by those who know you the best. Once you really open your mouth there is no doubt about your identity.

1 WEDNESDAY   *Moon Age Day 7 • Moon Sign Libra*

am ....

pm ....

The lunar low does not really take the wind out of your sails this time around because you don't really want to be blown anywhere. If you are content to wait and see, this could turn out to be an extremely enjoyable and fortunate sort of day. On the other hand there is frustration in trying to push a piece of rope!

2 THURSDAY   *Moon Age Day 8 • Moon Sign Libra*

am ....

pm ....

Others are a little difficult to deal with it's true. On the other hand you could simply leave them alone to get on with their own lives, whilst you sit in the middle of the field and blow the fluff from dandelion clocks. The field is probably metaphorical, but if you could find one, a real meadow would be even better.

3 FRIDAY

Moon Age Day 9 • Moon Sign Libra

am ....

pm ....

It could be rather difficult to push yourself to the forefront of any sort of activity at the moment, mainly because you don't really feel any need to do so. There are masses of small jobs piling up around you, but an equal number of enthusiastic friends and colleagues who will help you out.

4 SATURDAY

Moon Age Day 10 • Moon Sign Scorpio

am ....

pm ....

You can afford to be out socialising today, even though there are masses of things to be done in a practical sense. Not everyone seems to have your best interests at heart but since you are able to see through most individuals as if they were made of glass, this fact should not turn out to be a problem.

5 SUNDAY

Moon Age Day 11 • Moon Sign Scorpio

am ....

pm ....

The last push towards a chosen objective should leave you feeling more than pleased with yourself. In no way do you have to cheat another person out of anything in order to make gains yourself. The truth is rather the reverse because you carry your friends along on the journey to success.

← NEGATIVE TREND							POSITIVE TREND →				
-5	-4	-3	-2	-1			+1	+2	+3	+4	+5
					LOVE						
					MONEY						
					LUCK						
					VITALITY						

1998

YOUR MONTH AT A GLANCE

The twelve numbered boxes represent the important areas in your life. The key to the numbers you will find beneath the panel. A sun above the number indicates that opportunities are around. A cloud below the number, that you should be a bit defensive. Nothing above or below and life will be pretty ordinary.

1	2	3	4	5	6	7	8	9	10	11	12

JULY HIGHS AND LOWS

Here, I show how the rhythm of the Moon will affect you this month. Like the tide, your energies and abilities will rise and fall with its pattern. When it is above the date line, go-for-it. When it is below the line you should be resting.

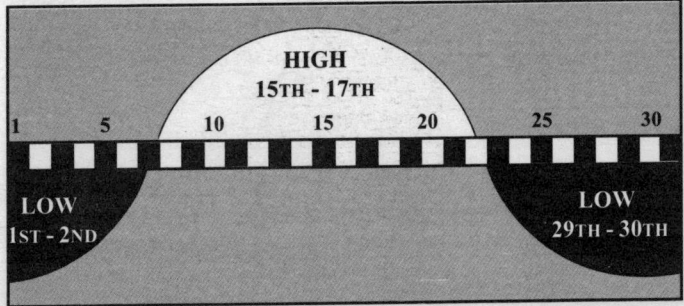

6 MONDAY
Moon Age Day 12 • Moon Sign Sagittarius

am ....

pm ....

You cannot afford to be left out of any social situation today, not only because you would miss the cut and thrust of human relationships but also on account of the personal needs that you have of them. Gains are made simply be being in the company of some progressive types, of which you are the most dynamic.

7 TUESDAY
Moon Age Day 13 • Moon Sign Sagittarius

am ....

pm ....

Don't expect all the opportunities of today to run quite as smoothly as you might wish It is only a matter of time before you are able to get rid of one or two less favourable trends, though in the meantime a little patience will be called for. It's a certain fact that there is no time for boredom however.

8 WEDNESDAY
Moon Age Day 14 • Moon Sign Sagittarius

am ....

pm ....

A more exciting atmosphere is discernible today and you are likely to follow up on one or two plans that have been put to one side recently. The influence you have over the lives of those around you is extremely well marked at present and you tend to act as a force for good when dealing with friends.

9 THURSDAY
Moon Age Day 15 • Moon Sign Capricorn

am ....

pm ....

There is some nostalgia about and you are certainly inclined to look back as well as forward today. This is probably no bad thing, just as long as you also bear in mind that you cannot use the past as a yardstick to the future in an exclusive sense. Rehearse a little speech before you appear in public.

10 FRIDAY   *Moon Age Day 16 • Moon Sign Capricorn*

am . . . .

pm . . . .

It isn't like you to stand in the background whilst others make the running, though you may have little choice but to do so with regard to a particular matter today. There is no shame in admitting that certain other people may sometimes know better than you do, which is the case for the moment.

11 SATURDAY   *Moon Age Day 17 • Moon Sign Aquarius*

am . . . .

pm . . . .

Teamwork is more or less guaranteed to get you where you want to go today and you are able to come to terms with certain people who have not always seen life your way in the past. It is likely that even where co-operation is the key to success, you feel yourself to be first amongst equals.

12 SUNDAY   *Moon Age Day 18 • Moon Sign Aquarius*

am . . . .

pm . . . .

The social and romantic aspects of life appeal to you more and more. Removing obstacles that have dogged your path previously you manage to smile through the whole of today and bring reluctant types round to your point of view. This is achieved without any bullying tactics and relies on your magnetic personality.

← *NEGATIVE TREND*								*POSITIVE TREND* →			
-5	-4	-3	-2	-1			+1	+2	+3	+4	+5
					LOVE						
					MONEY						
					LUCK						
					VITALITY						

13 MONDAY
Moon Age Day 19 • Moon Sign Pisces

am...

pm...

It may be necessary to settle the record concerning recent actions that you have taken. If there are any critics about they probably do not realise what your motivations were and it is up to you to make the situation plain. There is a chance to educate yourself into modes of thinking that have not been relevant before.

14 TUESDAY
Moon Age Day 20 • Moon Sign Pisces

am...

pm...

Although you can feel yourself to be rather impatient at the moment, the truth is that you are quite capable of waiting for opportunities to mature. This is what you have to do because there is absolutely no gain to be made from rushing your fences right now. A break from expected routines would be useful.

15 WEDNESDAY
Moon Age Day 21 • Moon Sign Aries

am...

pm...

With the Moon now firmly back in your sign you do everything you can to make the most of gains that have been accruing for a while. An entertaining interlude is at hand and some of the gains that are promised turn out to extend far beyond the period of the lunar high. Check matters out for yourself.

16 THURSDAY
Moon Age Day 22 • Moon Sign Aries

am...

pm...

With Lady Luck paying a call and all the promise of the month now at hand, you need to go out and get what you want. This certainly does not mean that you will be stepping on anyone's feet but you will have to be rather forceful if you want your nearest and dearest to make the same gains as you can.

17 FRIDAY   *Moon Age Day 23 • Moon Sign Aries*

am..

pm..

Things start to become a little more quiet as the day wears on, which is probably just as well if you want to have time to contemplate all that has been going on around you. Aries people who have decided to take this period for holidays may be the most fortunate of all because travel is just what you need.

18 SATURDAY   *Moon Age Day 24 • Moon Sign Taurus*

am..

pm..

The most charming side of your nature is almost certainly on display at present and you are able to make the most of social and personal encounters that seem to crop up of their own accord. Stop pushing so hard in a professional sense. For once you don't need to, and this is the weekend after all.

19 SUNDAY   *Moon Age Day 25 • Moon Sign Taurus*

am..

pm..

If you have it in mind to entertain at home, you could not pick a better time for doing so than this Sunday. People are only too willing to accept your invitations and you manage to bring a smile to a face that may not have known one for quite some time. Above all things at present, you are very funny.

← *NEGATIVE TREND*							*POSITIVE TREND* →			
-5	-4	-3	-2	-1		+1	+2	+3	+4	+5
					LOVE					
					MONEY					
					LUCK					
					VITALITY					

20 MONDAY
Moon Age Day 26 • Moon Sign Gemini

am . . . .

pm . . . .

Although you are probably not prepared at first to take the ideas of other people on board, there will come a time at some stage today when you will certainly consider doing so. There are various conflicting trends around just now so you may have to take the rough with the smooth, at least until the evening.

21 TUESDAY
Moon Age Day 27 • Moon Sign Gemini

am . . . .

pm . . . .

Activities out there in the wider world have a special appeal to you as this working week really begins to get going. There could be little enough time for social interaction, if only because there is so much to be done in a business sense. Even home based Arians will be constantly on the go.

22 WEDNESDAY
Moon Age Day 28 • Moon Sign Cancer

am . . . .

pm . . . .

If you discover that you have the opportunity today to settle a financial matter that has been on the boil for a while, you should not avoid doing so. Where a particular deal is concerned it is possible that you have made as much of matters as you can and this would be the best time to reap the reward.

23 THURSDAY
Moon Age Day 0 • Moon Sign Cancer

am . . . .

pm . . . .

You have a particularly unique view of life at present and can take any bull by the horns, just as long as you realise that there specific people around who genuinely do want to help you out on the way. If you find yourself involved in a controversy simply remember that your powers of discrimination are excellent now.

24 FRIDAY
Moon Age Day 1 • Moon Sign Leo

am ....

pm ....

A day when you feel you have the right to occupy a centre stage position and when others recognise the fact and would not try to better you. Although these trends are positive, it is worth allowing those with whom you work or live to know that they are of supreme importance to you.

25 SATURDAY
Moon Age Day 2 • Moon Sign Leo

am ....

pm ....

Are you sure that you are taking the opinions of others quite as seriously as you should? We all have flaws in our nature and one of yours tends to be that you 'know' things for others as well as for yourself. Perhaps you have better check with them. At least that way they know you are being considerate.

26 SUNDAY
Moon Age Day 3 • Moon Sign Virgo

am ....

pm ....

There is no doubt that you are highly industrious at the moment and so can get things done in no time at all. People come and go throughout the day and you have little or no time to converse with them about anything important. Perhaps you could save the evening to do just that. You need conversation today.

← NEGATIVE TREND						POSITIVE TREND →				
-5	-4	-3	-2	-1		+1	+2	+3	+4	+5
					LOVE					
					MONEY					
					LUCK					
					VITALITY					

27 MONDAY   *Moon Age Day 4 • Moon Sign Virgo*

am ....

pm ....

Whilst most people find you stimulating to have around, there may be one or two who are not so taken with your big personality. There is no pleasing everyone and the key day nature of today relies upon concentrating on those types who do find you attractive. You are able to cash in on their opinion.

28 TUESDAY   *Moon Age Day 5 • Moon Sign Virgo*

am ....

pm ....

Before the end of today you may start to notice some of the minor frustrations that mark the arrival of the Moon into your opposite sign. There are questions to be asked and today is an ideal time for putting them into words. Peace and happiness is what you are looking for, though finding it could be awkward.

29 WEDNESDAY   *Moon Age Day 6 • Moon Sign Libra*

am ....

pm ....

The lunar low is still around, and you simply have to make the best of the fact that you cannot move forward as quickly as you would wish all the time. If you have missed something important, you can always wait until it comes round again. This is certainly no time for crying over spilled milk.

30 THURSDAY   *Moon Age Day 7 • Moon Sign Libra*

am ....

pm ....

Difficulties ease out and you should find that today is at least moderately successful. Those who have some reason to rely on you do want to look after you at present and there is no harm at all in allowing yourself to be made the centre of attention. Concern over a friend may be misplaced.

31 FRIDAY ♦ *Moon Age Day 8 • Moon Sign Scorpio*

am ....

pm ....

Close emotional relationships capture your imagination today. Someone in the family, possibly a younger person, may show some tendency to rebel at present and the best way to deal with the situation is simply to be patient and wait. An air of mystery could fascinate you later in the day.

1 SATURDAY ♦ *Moon Age Day 9 • Moon Sign Scorpio*

am ....

pm ....

Hearth and home continues to be important to you at present and you find your greatest joy in the company of those people who mean the most to you. This could mean dropping the traces of responsibility and opting instead for a slower and more considered view of life and the way you are presently living it.

2 SUNDAY ♦ *Moon Age Day 10 • Moon Sign Sagittarius*

am ....

pm ....

There are things that cannot be explained in normal way, it's simply part of the way that the world works. Some deeply personal feelings find expression in some rather unusual ways right now and you can be certain that you have something of importance to say when you are listening to your inner mind.

← *NEGATIVE TREND*   *POSITIVE TREND* →

-5	-4	-3	-2	-1		+1	+2	+3	+4	+5
					LOVE					
					MONEY					
					LUCK					
					VITALITY					

1998

YOUR MONTH AT A GLANCE

The twelve numbered boxes represent the important areas in your life. The key to the numbers you will find beneath the panel. A sun above the number indicates that opportunities are around. A cloud below the number, that you should be a bit defensive. Nothing above or below and life will be pretty ordinary.

☀		☀			☀						
1	**2**	**3**	**4**	**5**	**6**	**7**	**8**	**9**	**10**	**11**	**12**
				☁							☁

AUGUST HIGHS AND LOWS

Here, I show how the rhythm of the Moon will affect you this month. Like the tide, your energies and abilities will rise and fall with its pattern. When it is above the date line, go-for-it. When it is below the line you should be resting.

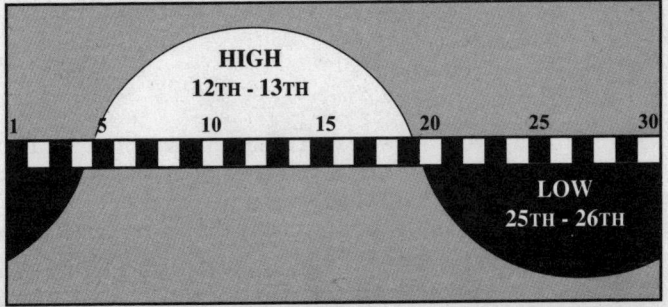

3 MONDAY ♦ *Moon Age Day 11 • Moon Sign Sagittarius*

am . . . .

pm . . . .

Opt for a change of scenery at any stage that this proves to be possible this week. Someone you will have your holidays planned for this month and you are certainly likely to be in the mood for a change at present. At work you should pace yourself, but not be too willing to take on extra responsibility.

4 TUESDAY ♦ *Moon Age Day 12 • Moon Sign Sagittarius*

am . . . .

pm . . . .

There may be some cause for celebrations at this time, not that you are likely to need an excuse whilst you are in your present frame of mind. In most respects this could be an excellent sort of day but it would be advisable not to over stretch yourself while personal enjoyments is promised.

5 WEDNESDAY ♦ *Moon Age Day 13 • Moon Sign Capricorn*

am . . . .

pm . . . .

You are productive and enterprising today. Although you are anxious to do as much as you can for those around you, the people in question might make this quite difficult. No matter how willing you are you can only do so much for people who are less than willing to help themselves on the way.

6 THURSDAY ♦ *Moon Age Day 14 • Moon Sign Capricorn*

am . . . .

pm . . . .

What sets this day apart is the way that others are so willing to allow you to have your head. This means that you are happy to take most of the decisions, whilst the world that keeps coming to your door is certain of the favours you can offer. Probably the sort of day that Aries tends to love the best.

7 FRIDAY   ♦   *Moon Age Day 15 • Moon Sign Aquarius*

am . . . .

pm . . . .

Keeping up a high social profile is both easy and important. In the main you should be feeling fairly good about yourself and will not be distracted by matters that could have been on your mind for a while now. As a result the generally positive trends do continue, if in a somewhat more subdued manner.

8 SATURDAY   ♦   *Moon Age Day 16 • Moon Sign Aquarius*

am . . . .

pm . . . .

Rehearse what you want to say at any given point in time and don't be afraid to speak your mind, even if you know that what you have to say is not going to be all that popular. You won't get anywhere by holding back and there are gains to be made from talking about the world as you see it.

9 SUNDAY   ♦   *Moon Age Day 17 • Moon Sign Aquarius*

am . . . .

pm . . . .

You may feel as if someone is trying to lead you up the garden path and since your own intuition tends to be your best guide at present, this is not a feeling that you should ignore. Not a good day for signing documents of any sort or for failing to read the small print on documents that you must deal with.

← *NEGATIVE TREND*										*POSITIVE TREND* →				
-5	-4	-3	-2	-1				+1	+2	+3	+4	+5
				LOVE							
				MONEY							
				LUCK							
				VITALITY							

10 MONDAY   ♦   *Moon Age Day 18 • Moon Sign Pisces*

am ....

pm ....

Beware of finding fault with those around you, for fear of making them look closer at your attitudes than they might otherwise tend to do. Some of you will be feeling a little tired, probably because you failed to get as much rest over the weekend as you might have done. Creative potential is good.

11 TUESDAY   ♦   *Moon Age Day 19 • Moon Sign Pisces*

am ....

pm ....

Although the day starts reasonably slowly it should not be long before you find most aspects speeding up considerably. You are looking at the arrival of the lunar high, which increases your powers of communication this time around and also strengthens your determination to do the right thing for you.

12 WEDNESDAY   ♦   *Moon Age Day 20 • Moon Sign Aries*

am ....

pm ....

Give and take are important at present, though it appears that those around you are only too happy to do most of the giving. Fortune smiles on you a little and there are offers around of both a professional and personal nature that you would not want to ignore. Confidence is certainly not lacking.

13 THURSDAY   ♦   *Moon Age Day 21 • Moon Sign Aries*

am ....

pm ....

With the lunar high still strong enough to have a bearing on your life, you might choose to take a little time out to spend as you would wish. The success of this day does not rely upon putting in all that much effort, but simply watching the trends that unfold and jumping on the bus of life at the right stop.

14 FRIDAY   ♦   *Moon Age Day 22 • Moon Sign Taurus*

am . . . .

pm . . . .

Trends go your way when it comes to speculations of some kind and you can afford to stick your neck out just a little. Arranging a social gathering might suit you right now and the end of the working week should bring with it the opportunity to stay out late and possibly to dance the night away.

15 SATURDAY   ♦   *Moon Age Day 23 • Moon Sign Taurus*

am . . . .

pm . . . .

Your secrets tend to be safe with friends, whilst colleagues and people you do not know all that well are probably not so reliable at present. If you have something really important on your mind it might be best to save it until the evening, when you can turn to a loved on you trust quite implicitly.

16 SUNDAY   ♦   *Moon Age Day 24 • Moon Sign Gemini*

am . . . .

pm . . . .

Instant decisions are called for, even in situations that are not of a practical nature at all. Thus you could be called upon to arrange a trip at short notice, or to attend some sort of function that has been arranged at the last minute. Whatever you do, enjoy any good weather that this Sunday brings and choose variety.

← *NEGATIVE TREND*						*POSITIVE TREND*	→			
-5	-4	-3	-2	-1		+1	+2	+3	+4	+5
					LOVE					
					MONEY					
					LUCK					
					VITALITY					

17 MONDAY ♦ *Moon Age Day 25 • Moon Sign Gemini*

am...

pm...

Your powers of attraction are extremely high during the working week that lies ahead, but probably never more so than today. Acting on impulse is part of what you are and there is every opportunity to exploit this potential at present. You are less likely to run into problems as a result of being impetuous.

18 TUESDAY ♦ *Moon Age Day 26 • Moon Sign Cancer*

am...

pm...

You will be expected to take part in discussions and to bring a breath of fresh air to situations that need just your sort of positive touch. It is possible that you will be amazed at the level of attention that is being paid to your opinions, though on the other hand you are very confident through most of this week.

19 WEDNESDAY ♦ *Moon Age Day 27 • Moon Sign Cancer*

am...

pm...

There is a slight tendency for you to take others for granted today, even your nearest and dearest, who are doing all they can to be of service to you. Not a time for getting bogged down with jobs that you may start, but which you will not find yourself able or willing to finish.

20 THURSDAY ♦ *Moon Age Day 28 • Moon Sign Leo*

am...

pm...

If there is an initiative to be taken today, you are the person for it. This Thursday brings the chance of a change of scene, and of attitude. People crop up in your life who turn out to be distinctly intriguing and you will want to get to know them as soon as possible. Don't make loved ones jealous though.

21 FRIDAY ♦ *Moon Age Day 0 • Moon Sign Leo*

am . . . .

pm . . . .

Leaving things until the last minute may not be the right way to proceed today. This is really not your way of dealing with matters in any case, since you are usually much more likely to pitch in and have a go right at the start of any enterprise. Better not to get involved at all than to procrastinate later.

22 SATURDAY ♦ *Moon Age Day 1 • Moon Sign Leo*

am . . . .

pm . . . .

Obstacles exist to be overcome in your life today and you should not be hesitant about tackling them head on. You cannot get away from the needs that certain other people have of you, though once you have tackled them you should be glad that you were around to do so. Love is on your mind today.

23 SUNDAY ♦ *Moon Age Day 2 • Moon Sign Virgo*

am . . . .

pm . . . .

As the Sun enters your solar sixth house, so you find that career matters are on your mind. Of course this might not be much use on a Sunday, but you do have the advantage of thinking clearly today, and the time to lay down some important plans for the future. You are storing up your gold quietly.

← NEGATIVE TREND							POSITIVE TREND →			
-5	-4	-3	-2	-1		+1	+2	+3	+4	+5
					LOVE					
					MONEY					
					LUCK					
					VITALITY					

24 MONDAY
Moon Age Day 3 • Moon Sign Virgo

am ....

pm ....

A day when you need to look at the potential that lies at the heart of any particular happening, whilst refusing to be dazzled by the light of the thing itself. A subtle approach works best, and this is something that you sometimes fail to understand. Any tendency to be tired should soon evaporate like the morning mist.

25 TUESDAY
Moon Age Day 4 • Moon Sign Libra

am ....

pm ....

Stand up for what you believe in if you want others to do the same on your behalf. This is certainly no time to stand in the shadows, which may be what you are inclined to do because of the presence of the lunar low. Some extra push and self belief is called for, and you are the person to find it in yourself.

26 WEDNESDAY
Moon Age Day 5 • Moon Sign Libra

am ....

pm ....

Probably a quieter day than of late, though not necessarily difficult or tedious as a result. Actions tend to speak louder than words when you are in the company of people who are of supreme importance to you, whilst a great deal of patience at a personal level will pay handsome dividends eventually.

27 THURSDAY
Moon Age Day 6 • Moon Sign Libra

am ....

pm ....

If it seems that you get stuck on and off today, keep changing direction. There is nothing like making others guess what your next move might be if you want to keep their attention focused on you. It is possible that you have a fairly high opinion of your capabilities at the present time.

28 FRIDAY   *Moon Age Day 7 • Moon Sign Scorpio*

am . . . .

pm . . . .

Minor complications look as though they might get in the way, but fail to
do so when the chips are down. Talking about chips, this could be a good
time for chancing your luck a little, though only if you are certain about
the odds and if you know that the game is rigged to favour you .

29 SATURDAY   *Moon Age Day 8 • Moon Sign Scorpio*

am . . . .

pm . . . .

Work is put onto the back burner, and especially so if this is the start of
your holiday week. Even if it isn't you can behave as if it should be. Please
yourself, have a good time and make certain that you stay away from
pressure or tension just as much as you can, from the start of the day until
its close.

30 SUNDAY   *Moon Age Day 9 • Moon Sign Sagittarius*

am . . . .

pm . . . .

Although it is sometimes rather boring keeping to tried and tested paths,
this is what you are best at doing right now. Confidence tends to be fairly
high, but should not be squandered on situations that can never be
turned to your advantage, no matter how much you think you would want
them to be.

← NEGATIVE TREND							POSITIVE TREND →				
-5	-4	-3	-2	-1			+1	+2	+3	+4	+5
					LOVE						
					MONEY						
					LUCK						
					VITALITY						

31 MONDAY   *Moon Age Day 10 • Moon Sign Sagittarius*

am ....

pm ....

The start of a new working week marks the end of the month and there is so much pleasure coming your way that you should be certain to look towards September with a degree of optimism and enthusiasm. Don't try to burn the candle at both ends because it is personal pleasure that counts now.

1 TUESDAY   *Moon Age Day 11 • Moon Sign Sagittarius*

am ....

pm ....

Career and personal projects are now on your mind and you experience what should be another very productive and potentially successful sort of day. The attitude of friends and family alike does not leave you guessing and so it is possible to negotiate the twists and turns of life quite easily.

2 WEDNESDAY   *Moon Age Day 12 • Moon Sign Capricorn*

am ....

pm ....

All manner of rules and regulations are inclined to get on your nerves at this time, which is why you may decide to take a break from the normal path your life is set upon. You can surprise others, simply by adopting an alternative strategy. It may not last, but your objectives are achieved all the same.

3 THURSDAY   *Moon Age Day 13 • Moon Sign Capricorn*

am ....

pm ....

Compromise is the important word in your life today, even though as a rule it does not appear in your own personal dictionary. There is support available today that you really need and you only have access to it if you are willing to let others know they are doing a good job too. It doesn't hurt to be complimentary.

4 FRIDAY   *Moon Age Day 14 • Moon Sign Aquarius*

am...

pm...

You could find yourself being rather dominant in your treatment of family members. Although this is not always the best way to proceed, if you have thought matters through very carefully, it might just be necessary to bulldoze an idea or opinion through. You do have their best interests at heart after all.

5 SATURDAY   *Moon Age Day 15 • Moon Sign Aquarius*

am...

pm...

Although you are not doing so deliberately, there is a chance that you are making life rather miserable for others. Stop and think who might be suffering as a result of your present ideas and attitudes and modify them if you know that you are stepping on someone's toes. It's never too late to learn.

6 SUNDAY   *Moon Age Day 16 • Moon Sign Pisces*

am...

pm...

There is a positive balance between what you want from life and the way that circumstances arrange themselves at present. You pick up on the connections and turn them to your advantage at every turn. If you cannot really understand why, it does not matter because things happen in any case.

← *NEGATIVE TREND*							*POSITIVE TREND*		→	
-5	-4	-3	-2	-1		+1	+2	+3	+4	+5
					LOVE					
					MONEY					
					LUCK					
					VITALITY					

1998

YOUR MONTH AT A GLANCE

The twelve numbered boxes represent the important areas in your life. The key to the numbers you will find beneath the panel. A sun above the number indicates that opportunities are around. A cloud below the number, that you should be a bit defensive. Nothing above or below and life will be pretty ordinary.

1	2	3	4	5	6	7	8	9	10	11	12

SEPTEMBER HIGHS AND LOWS

Here, I show how the rhythm of the Moon will affect you this month. Like the tide, your energies and abilities will rise and fall with its pattern. When it is above the date line, go-for-it. When it is below the line you should be resting.

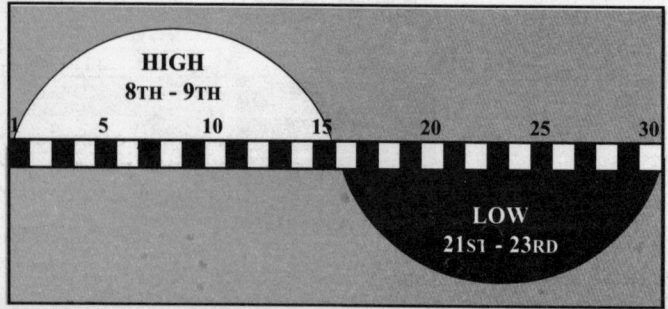

7 MONDAY

Moon Age Day 17 • Moon Sign Pisces

am ....

pm ....

You are very trusting of others today, so much so that you may get your fingers burned unless you check out the facts and figures of situations carefully. Anxious to do your best for everyone, you move forward plans that really ought to wait until you are in a more positive frame of mind.

8 TUESDAY

Moon Age Day 18 • Moon Sign Aries

am ....

pm ....

With the lunar high comes a definite surge in energy and the determination to take life by the scruff of the neck. There is little to hold you back at the moment and if there is a problem today it is likely to be that you are working a little harder than you really need to. Personalities could enter your life.

9 WEDNESDAY

Moon Age Day 19 • Moon Sign Aries

am ....

pm ....

New projects, invitations and offers of new romantic attachments, all could play an important part in your life at the present time. Not everyone works the same way you do, but it really does not seem to matter all that much at present. Keep a close ear to the ground when it comes to professional matters.

10 THURSDAY

Moon Age Day 20 • Moon Sign Taurus

am ....

pm ....

You have a unique ability to get your own way most of the time, but never more so than right now. A sense of proportion is probably very important, but since you are not the sort of person to cultivate such a thing as a rule, it is not likely that you are able to do so now with any startling success.

11 FRIDAY

Moon Age Day 21 • Moon Sign Taurus

am . . . .

pm . . . .

If there is any careful planning to be done, this is a day for getting down to it. Before you embark upon any new project it would be very sensible to make certain that you have thought matters through to their logical conclusion. If you feel that you need some timely advice, it should be on offer.

12 SATURDAY

Moon Age Day 22 • Moon Sign Gemini

am . . . .

pm . . . .

This could be the least favourable part of the month for making any sort of snap decisions. On the whole you would be better off sticking to tried and tested paths and leaving the more exciting personal or financial possibilities until a little further down the line. An advantage is gained in a domestic matter.

13 SUNDAY

Moon Age Day 23 • Moon Sign Gemini

am . . . .

pm . . . .

Out of the confusion that aspects of your personal life seems to be at present comes forth a degree of order that might surprise you. This could be due to the very real efforts of your partner or a close friend and you need to listen carefully to what they are suggesting. Don't be too ready to take the blame.

← NEGATIVE TREND						POSITIVE TREND		→		
-5	-4	-3	-2	-1		+1	+2	+3	+4	+5
					LOVE					
					MONEY					
					LUCK					
					VITALITY					

14 MONDAY

Moon Age Day 24 • Moon Sign Cancer

am ....

pm ....

It looks as though you are going to be a little more fussy about matters concerning domestic arrangements than would normally be the case and that means looking very carefully at your own behaviour before you do anything that cannot be undone. Major decisions are, quite frankly, best left for now.

15 TUESDAY

Moon Age Day 25 • Moon Sign Cancer

am ....

pm ....

Chances are that you work with great efficiency at present and that you will be making it plain to almost everyone just how much you want life to run smoothly. Whether or not they are willing to believe you does remain to be seen. In the main your sincerity should show and you have good persuasive skills.

16 WEDNESDAY

Moon Age Day 26 • Moon Sign Cancer

am ....

pm ....

Although the expectations that you have of yourself and the world at large tend to be fairly high at present, there is no reason to believe that you will come unstuck. Just keep plodding along in your own sweet way at work and don't allow yourself to be pushed into any sort of corner in terms of personal matters.

17 THURSDAY

Moon Age Day 27 • Moon Sign Leo

am ....

pm ....

There are many different sorts of people about today and all of them have something to say to you. You really will have to slow things down a little so that you find the time and incentive to listen to words of wisdom. This is a commodity that is not exclusively your monopoly and the truth can come from almost anywhere.

18 FRIDAY

Moon Age Day 28 • Moon Sign Leo

am . . . .

pm . . . .

You are prepared to put in some long, hard hours if that is what it takes to get what you really want from life. All the same it would be no bad thing to take a journey if the chance to do so comes along and the opportunity would be especially good in setting you up for the harder months of winter that lie ahead.

19 SATURDAY

Moon Age Day 29 • Moon Sign Virgo

am . . . .

pm . . . .

You are still looking for a change of routine, even if this only turns out to be a fairly low key sort of affair. Reasoned argument works best when you are trying to get your own way at home, though there is every reason that other family members have the same basic needs and desires that you do.

20 SUNDAY

Moon Age Day 0 • Moon Sign Virgo

am . . . .

pm . . . .

Turning from a situation when you really were not sure what job you should tackle next, you now manage to get most matters sorted out ahead of yourself, so that life seems to take on a rather more logical look than it has in recent days. Your general sense of excitement is aroused, and this makes you think.

← NEGATIVE TREND								POSITIVE TREND →				
-5	-4	-3	-2	-1			+1	+2	+3	+4	+5
					LOVE						
					MONEY						
					LUCK						
					VITALITY						

21 MONDAY   *Moon Age Day 1 • Moon Sign Libra*

am ....

pm ....

Confidence is everything to you at present and there is no lack of determination to get exactly what you want from most professional situations. All the same there is no reason to run yourself ragged, especially at a time when you will want to be turning at least part of your mind to personal enjoyment.

22 TUESDAY   *Moon Age Day 2 • Moon Sign Libra*

am ....

pm ....

The lunar low is still inclined to slow things down a little, which leaves pause for thought and a time when you will be thinking about plans for several weeks or months ahead. A long term strategy is no bad thing to have, and although you often change from day to day, you can at least bear it in mind.

23 WEDNESDAY   *Moon Age Day 3 • Moon Sign Libra*

am ....

pm ....

As the Sun sails into your solar seventh house you find that to work in pairs turns out to be very useful. Often you are a solo operator, though this is much less likely to be the case in the four week period that lies before you. There are some fairly startling lessons to be learned through co-operation.

24 THURSDAY   *Moon Age Day 4 • Moon Sign Scorpio*

am ....

pm ....

With Mercury coming especially strong for you at present there is every reason to think that you should be saying exactly what you feel. In the public arena you are versatile and inclined to say the first thing that comes into your head. This should be cautioned against as a rule, but not for you right now.

153

25 FRIDAY

Moon Age Day 5 • Moon Sign Scorpio

am . . . .

pm . . . .

You have to get to the root of matters in an emotional sense if you are to make any real sense of them later. Up and about early in the day you opt for a period of exploration, especially when it comes to understanding what makes you tick at a fairly deep level. Nobody tends to get in your way however.

26 SATURDAY

Moon Age Day 6 • Moon Sign Sagittarius

am . . . .

pm . . . .

Once again you are in the mood for travel and would not take kindly to be stopped in your tracks if you get the urge to move around. In all probability most types would be willing to go along for the ride. Look out for an unexpected but quite exciting romantic interlude that beckons at some stage.

27 SUNDAY

Moon Age Day 7 • Moon Sign Sagittarius

am . . . .

pm . . . .

A good time for shining a light on an issue that had definitely been in the dark for some weeks or months. This is made possible as a result of something that is being said to you by an outside agency and could come about thanks to the most casual of conversations that is made possible by a restful Sunday.

← *NEGATIVE TREND*							*POSITIVE TREND* →				
-5	-4	-3	-2	-1			+1	+2	+3	+4	+5
					LOVE						
					MONEY						
					LUCK						
					VITALITY						

28 MONDAY   *Moon Age Day 8 • Moon Sign Sagittarius*

am . . . .

pm . . . .

What you know at the commencement of this working week, you know absolutely. A small word of caution however because not everyone has quite the faith in you that you have in yourself. Not a period for allowing yourself to think about personal matters too deeply, since you do not need restricting.

29 TUESDAY   *Moon Age Day 9 • Moon Sign Capricorn*

am . . . .

pm . . . .

What a good period this should be in terms of personal relationships. You can get more or less whatever you want from one-to-one attachments and should be allowing the more imaginative qualities of your deeply sensual nature to have their way. Comfort and security are of supreme interest too right now.

30 WEDNESDAY   *Moon Age Day 10 • Moon Sign Capricorn*

am . . . .

pm . . . .

Once again relationships loom large in your estimation of what is on offer and you manage to say just the right things at the correct time. Highly charged at present, it is unlikely that you would misconstrue the feelings of another person, so once you have made your mind up, you can really go for gold.

1 THURSDAY   *Moon Age Day 11 • Moon Sign Aquarius*

am . . . .

pm . . . .

There is a strong need for company today, but probably not on the same terms as has been the case during the last few days. Now you want the general association of many individuals and intimacy is less well accented. Such trends can help you at work, where colleagues have an important part to play.

2 FRIDAY

Moon Age Day 12 • Moon Sign Aquarius

am ....

pm ....

Don't expect an easy going sort of day, though that does not mean that you fail to enjoy what is on offer at this time. Arguments should be avoided at all cost because they do nothing to serve your best interests at the moment. Rules and regulations get on your nerves and you could be ignoring them.

3 SATURDAY

Moon Age Day 13 • Moon Sign Pisces

am ....

pm ....

Beware of the sort of advice that is coming from your immediate circle. It is not that anyone is deliberately trying to mislead you, simply that the information that they are working on themselves is not especially reliable. Think about the sheer logic of any situation before you act or react.

4 SUNDAY

Moon Age Day 14 • Moon Sign Pisces

am ....

pm ....

A gentle approach works best when you are dealing with loved ones, many of whom may have been through a fairly trying time of late. Wherever it is that you want to go in a personal sense, there should be no real rush about how you get there. Entertainment captures your imagination during this Sunday.

← *NEGATIVE TREND*								*POSITIVE TREND* →				
-5	-4	-3	-2	-1				+1	+2	+3	+4	+5
					LOVE							
					MONEY							
					LUCK							
					VITALITY							

1998

YOUR MONTH AT A GLANCE

The twelve numbered boxes represent the important areas in your life. The key to the numbers you will find beneath the panel. A sun above the number indicates that opportunities are around. A cloud below the number, that you should be a bit defensive. Nothing above or below and life will be pretty ordinary.

1	2	3	4	5	6	7	8	9	10	11	12
☀	☀	☀									
						☁			☁		

KEY

1 Strength of Personality
2 Personal Finance
3 Useful Information Gathering
4 Domestic Affairs
5 Pleasure & Romance
6 Effective Work & Health

7 One to One Relationships
8 Questioning, Thinking & Deciding
9 External Influences / Education
10 Career Aspirations
11 Teamwork Activities
12 Unconscious Impulses

OCTOBER HIGHS AND LOWS

Here, I show how the rhythm of the Moon will affect you this month. Like the tide, your energies and abilities will rise and fall with its pattern. When it is above the date line, go-for-it. When it is below the line you should be resting.

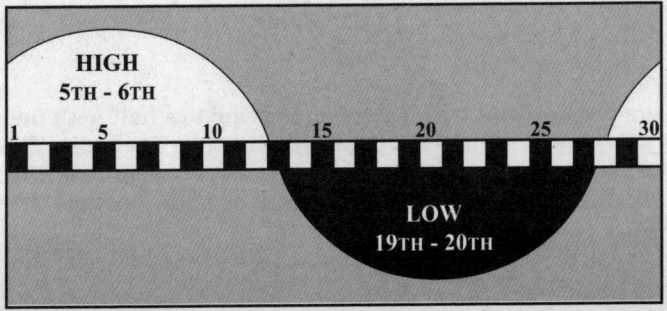

5 MONDAY
Moon Age Day 15 • Moon Sign Aries

am ....

pm ....

It should not be at all difficult to get yourself into gear today. The Moon is back in your sign and all sorts of gains are there for the taking. Be bold in your dealings with the world at large, and especially so at work, where you are being watched carefully by people who are in a position to help you.

6 TUESDAY
Moon Age Day 16 • Moon Sign Aries

am ....

pm ....

Look at restrictions very carefully today because it is more than likely that even these can be turned to your advantage. Key days are useful for getting around, over or through potential traps that have been a problem to you in the past. None of them last very long under the present trends.

7 WEDNESDAY
Moon Age Day 17 • Moon Sign Taurus

am ....

pm ....

Chances are that you still feel on top of the world this morning and will be anxious to put all the energy you can into new and interesting projects that have a bearing on the more practical aspects of life. Gains are often far ahead of you, but you have your own telescope on the future and see them clearly.

8 THURSDAY
Moon Age Day 18 • Moon Sign Taurus

am ....

pm ....

There are people about who may seem to grind to a halt with their own efforts today and it is up to you to get them back on line again. This does not take up too much of your time and turns out to offer new incentives that provide you with new material for your own life. An ideal time to be of service.

9 FRIDAY
Moon Age Day 19 • Moon Sign Gemini

am ....

pm ....

You are a conduit for new ideas, both those you dream up for yourself and the sort that are still coming from people in your vicinity. Give and take are equally important in a personal sense and you need to feel that there is very real interaction going on throughout every sphere of your life.

10 SATURDAY
Moon Age Day 20 • Moon Sign Gemini

am ....

pm ....

Although you tend to nanny those you care about the most, chances are that this is not what they want and so you might as well save yourself the time. If you do, the possibilities that come about as a result of better communication and a more determined attitude soon make themselves known today.

11 SUNDAY
Moon Age Day 21 • Moon Sign Gemini

am ....

pm ....

Stay around people and situations that you know the best because there is just a small chance that you are not quite as confident today as you have been of late. This is a very short interlude and arriving on a Sunday, some of you may not even notice it at all. The best of times for simply having a rest.

← NEGATIVE TREND					POSITIVE TREND →				
-5	-4	-3	-2	-1	+1	+2	+3	+4	+5
LOVE									
MONEY									
LUCK									
VITALITY									

12 MONDAY

Moon Age Day 22 • Moon Sign Cancer

am ....

pm ....

Once again you are fully back into the swing of life and very keen to make a favourable impression on just about anyone you come into contact with. The key day possibilities of today come about as a result of personal relationships, which look secure, happy and generally on line.

13 TUESDAY

Moon Age Day 23 • Moon Sign Cancer

am ....

pm ....

Don't get so wrapped up in your own emotional considerations that you fail to notice what is going on around you in the family. Friends also have a strong need of you, which is a fact of life throughout most of this month. The day is better than average but passion could be lacking where you had expected it to be.

14 WEDNESDAY

Moon Age Day 24 • Moon Sign Leo

am ....

pm ....

Both social and love matters bring you much of what you are searching for, even if you have to wait a little longer than you might wish. You need to take the traces of your own destiny in your hands, but that does not mean that you need to try and arrange every single detail of your life entirely on your own.

15 THURSDAY

Moon Age Day 25 • Moon Sign Leo

am ....

pm ....

Partnerships seem to be working especially well today and if you have the chance to co-operate at work you should not turn down the possibility simply because you think you have all the ideas. There are few difficulties to deal with at the moment, but probably little real progress either.

16 FRIDAY   *Moon Age Day 26 • Moon Sign Virgo*

am . . . .

pm . . . .

An issue that has previously arisen only between yourself and others now falls into the public domain. Anything could be the start that sparks off a clash of personalities, and that is really what you have to be aware of now. If you refuse to be involved in deep discussions, you can side-step any potential problem.

17 SATURDAY   *Moon Age Day 27 • Moon Sign Virgo*

am . . . .

pm . . . .

There is a very competitive side to you at present, which is not really surprising considering that you come from the most progressive and dynamic sign of the zodiac. A political stance won't really help, though you are almost certain to cross swords with someone, unless of course you keep to yourself.

18 SUNDAY   *Moon Age Day 28 • Moon Sign Virgo*

am . . . .

pm . . . .

Things slow down, and with the lunar low in sight it would be better to use these trends rather than to worry about them. The simple fact is that you can look at life, turn your attention to the longer-term future and hold back on the sort of activity that is hard to justify and which doesn't appeal at present.

← NEGATIVE TREND							POSITIVE TREND →			
-5	-4	-3	-2	-1			+1	+2	+3	+4	+5
					LOVE					
					MONEY					
					LUCK					
					VITALITY					

19 MONDAY
Moon Age Day 29 • Moon Sign Libra

am ....

pm ....

Don't expect everything to go your way. Actually the strength of these trends really depend on what it is you are trying to achieve. It's impossible to push a piece of rope and that is exactly what you seem to be doing if you are determined to make progress today. Better by far to take a break from efforts.

20 TUESDAY
Moon Age Day 0 • Moon Sign Libra

am ....

pm ....

Whilst general relationships seem to be going fairly well, there is one potential attachment which looks especially good. Remove yourself from any situation that is certain to cause discussions or arguments, neither of which you need at present. You need to diversify for the best chance of success now.

21 WEDNESDAY
Moon Age Day 1 • Moon Sign Scorpio

am ....

pm ....

You should find family members easy to deal with and only too willing to see what you are certain is a sensible point of view. Because of this you should spend at least a small part of today putting into place changes of a domestic nature that have been on your mind for a while. Love conquers slight problems.

22 THURSDAY
Moon Age Day 2 • Moon Sign Scorpio

am ....

pm ....

It is possible that you are in too much of a hurry to put the finishing touches to certain projects that are going to be of supreme importance in a week or two. So often you only really get yourself into gear when it is absolutely necessary, yet you can save yourself much effort later by acting with determination now.

23 FRIDAY   *Moon Age Day 3 • Moon Sign Scorpio*

am . . . .

pm . . . .

A sense of renewal comes about, mainly thanks to the much better powers of discrimination of friends and colleagues. Contingencies that you have put into place in the past now show themselves to have been eminently sensible. Anything too serious or contentious will probably be avoided for the moment.

24 SATURDAY   *Moon Age Day 4 • Moon Sign Sagittarius*

am . . . .

pm . . . .

Whilst certain aspects of your life as a whole could seem to be restrictive, the mainstream of events point you onward and forward this weekend. Standard responses to the needs of personal relationships don't work all that well, which is why you push up the pace and turn to greater excitement.

25 SUNDAY   *Moon Age Day 5 • Moon Sign Sagittarius*

am . . . .

pm . . . .

Opt for as much variety as possible today and make this a Sunday to remember. There will probably be time to sort out a slight financial quirk that has existed for some weeks and to do so should put your mind at rest. Not everyone is easy to deal with, but most of your closest friends set out to please you.

← NEGATIVE TREND							POSITIVE TREND →				
-5	-4	-3	-2	-1			+1	+2	+3	+4	+5
					LOVE						
					MONEY						
					LUCK						
					VITALITY						

26 MONDAY   *Moon Age Day 6 • Moon Sign Capricorn*

am ....

pm ....

Certain career moves can be contemplated much more realistically now than has been the case for quite a while. This process is assisted by the fact that offers actually come to you, rather than you having to search them out. Charity minded Arians are really coming into their own under prevailing trends.

27 TUESDAY   *Moon Age Day 7 • Moon Sign Capricorn*

am ....

pm ....

Improvements to your life come about on the back of recent activities and a sense of enterprise. For the first time this month Lady Luck should really be on your side and you may not have to do all that much to find gains are obvious. Confidence is the key to success and there is no lack of it.

28 WEDNESDAY   *Moon Age Day 8 • Moon Sign Capricorn*

am ....

pm ....

Select the friendships that you know to be the best ones for everyone concerned, even if this means that one or two people fall into the background at this stage. Stay in the midst of exciting potentials and do your best to get an idea across to colleagues that has been on your mind for ages.

29 THURSDAY   *Moon Age Day 9 • Moon Sign Aquarius*

am ....

pm ....

Take it nice and easy today. You do not have to flog yourself to make headway in life and also need to realise that there is no harm in gaining from effort you have put in previously. There is a time to push ahead and a period for stopping to watch the flowers grow. Even in October the latter applies now.

30 FRIDAY   *Moon Age Day 10 • Moon Sign Aquarius*

am . . . .

pm . . . .

Today may present you with the biggest challenge for quite some time. What form this takes in entirely dependent on your personal circumstances, though there is little doubt that you would notice the opportunities that surround you. The advice is simple: take the bull by the horns and be a typical Aries subject.

31 SATURDAY   *Moon Age Day 11 • Moon Sign Pisces*

am . . . .

pm . . . .

Although you may feel slightly lacking in sparkle today, that does not mean that you appear to be dull when seen through the eyes of other people. For this reason you will not find today to be good for looking in the mirror. Only what the world at large thinks about you really counts at the end of the day.

1 SUNDAY   *Moon Age Day 12 • Moon Sign Pisces*

am . . . .

pm . . . .

The first day of November finds your Moon growing closer to Aries again. Tomorrow represents a possible turning point and works better for you if you have thought matters through carefully now. You tend to direct your life's ship best from the Pilot's seat today, so let others set the sails.

← *NEGATIVE TREND*   *POSITIVE TREND* →

-5	-4	-3	-2	-1		+1	+2	+3	+4	+5
					LOVE	▓	▓	▓		
					MONEY	▓	▓			
					LUCK			▓		
					VITALITY	▓				

1998

YOUR MONTH AT A GLANCE

The twelve numbered boxes represent the important areas in your life. The key to the numbers you will find beneath the panel. A sun above the number indicates that opportunities are around. A cloud below the number, that you should be a bit defensive. Nothing above or below and life will be pretty ordinary.

1	2	3	4	5	6	7	8	9	10	11	12

KEY

1 Strength of Personality	7 One to One Relationships
2 Personal Finance	8 Questioning, Thinking & Deciding
3 Useful Information Gathering	9 External Influences / Education
4 Domestic Affairs	10 Career Aspirations
5 Pleasure & Romance	11 Teamwork Activities
6 Effective Work & Health	12 Unconscious Impulses

NOVEMBER HIGHS AND LOWS

Here, I show how the rhythm of the Moon will affect you this month. Like the tide, your energies and abilities will rise and fall with its pattern. When it is above the date line, go-for-it. When it is below the line you should be resting.

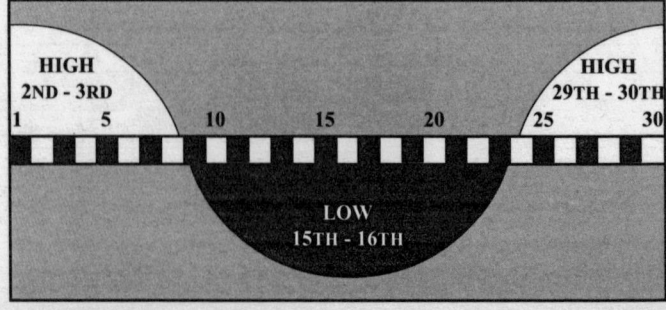

2 MONDAY
Moon Age Day 13 • Moon Sign Aries

am ....

pm ....

Things are on line for a powerful and interesting day. There are times when the lunar high is especially potent in your life and it looks as though this is one of them. An entertaining interlude, when you can not only have more or less what you want from life, but also enjoy seeking it out.

3 TUESDAY
Moon Age Day 14 • Moon Sign Aries

am ....

pm ....

One or two matters could be rather up in the air today, but what do you care? The truth is that you have plenty to keep you occupied and that you should be more than happy with the general progress that you are making at present. Financial matters may be sorted out to your satisfaction at this time.

4 WEDNESDAY
Moon Age Day 15 • Moon Sign Taurus

am ....

pm ....

Certain aspects of your life deserve a little special attention at the moment. Personal matters are probably on your mind, especially if loved ones are not behaving in quite the way you have come to expect. Arguing for your limitations means that you could find them, so it's important to be quite confident.

5 THURSDAY
Moon Age Day 16 • Moon Sign Taurus

am ....

pm ....

Once again confidence is the key, even if you do not really feel that you have quite as much of that elusive quality as you may wish. A return to older values might be useful, particularly since you have time to look at matters more closely today. Not everything you did previously is old fashioned now!

6 FRIDAY
Moon Age Day 17 • Moon Sign Gemini

am ....

pm ....

Try to stay away from undertaking several different tasks at the same time because you may only serve to confuse yourself on the way. There is time to take it easy, especially later in the day and although bright lights and the possibility of enjoyment seem to beckon in one way, in another you feel like resting.

7 SATURDAY
Moon Age Day 18 • Moon Sign Gemini

am ....

pm ....

The weekend brings a change of scenery or an alteration in attitude. You cannot really expect to be thinking about personal matters in the way that you did last year, or even last week. The truth is that we all change as we go along, a fact that you mind find necessary to explain to someone you care for deeply.

8 SUNDAY
Moon Age Day 19 • Moon Sign Cancer

am ....

pm ....

Don't allow the attitude of a family member to divert you from something that you know to be absolutely necessary. Energy and determination are present in equal quantity, just as long as you bear in mind that this is a Sunday and that there is no reason to push yourself too hard. Family routines tend to be welcome.

← *NEGATIVE TREND*						*POSITIVE TREND* →				
-5	-4	-3	-2	-1		+1	+2	+3	+4	+5
					LOVE					
					MONEY					
					LUCK					
					VITALITY					

9 MONDAY
Moon Age Day 20 • Moon Sign Cancer

am . . . .

pm . . . .

Small disappointments at work could have more of a bearing on your life than is strictly fair or necessary at present. An entertaining time is likely once you have left the cares and worries of life behind and you do what you can to perk up the general spirits of family members, some of whom are a little depressed.

10 TUESDAY
Moon Age Day 21 • Moon Sign Leo

am . . . .

pm . . . .

Someone, and probably more than one person, is in the right place and the correct frame of mind to do you a good turn. Avoid turning away from such a possibility on account of pride, or you may forgo the benefits of this key day. You are only reaping the harvest that you have sown in the past.

11 WEDNESDAY
Moon Age Day 22 • Moon Sign Leo

am . . . .

pm . . . .

It looks as though this is going to be a high point in personal terms, with plenty to keep you occupied and little or no tendency to be held back. Energy is present when you need it, but for much of the time you are coasting along and living off the glory that you have managed to create through most of the year.

12 THURSDAY
Moon Age Day 23 • Moon Sign Virgo

am . . . .

pm . . . .

Important discussions of a practical nature should not be overlooked at this time. You are in the mood for having a good time too, so you will not want to be talking the entire day away, unless what is being said has a happy and recreational twist to it. Friends have a definite desire to please you.

13 FRIDAY
Moon Age Day 24 • Moon Sign Virgo

am ....

pm ....

You probably never felt more wanted than turns out to be the case today. This is the special nature of present trends, that you come to understand just how very important you are to those around you. Not a time for thinking too much about finances, or matters that are difficult to control at present.

14 SATURDAY
Moon Age Day 25 • Moon Sign Virgo

am ....

pm ....

Take some time out and think about life for a change. There isn't a great deal that you can do to change anything right now and you would be much better off simply allowing yourself to drift on the tide. What else can you do when the lunar low is about to arrive? A fairly happy day if you do not fret.

15 SUNDAY
Moon Age Day 26 • Moon Sign Libra

am ....

pm ....

Although life still tends to be quiet you can get on with a whole series of new possibilities that relate to creative potential. Frustrations only attend you if you are determined to deal with practicalities that really should wait. The ultimate success you seek is hidden, but only for a day or two.

← NEGATIVE TREND						POSITIVE TREND →				
-5	-4	-3	-2	-1		+1	+2	+3	+4	+5
					LOVE					
					MONEY					
					LUCK					
					VITALITY					

16 MONDAY   *Moon Age Day 27 • Moon Sign Libra*

am ....

pm ....

Little by little today it appears that the prospects for your life generally are on the up. The reversal of the lunar low trends leaves you feeling more confident. but that does not mean trying to be at your most dynamic, for today at least. A steady acceleration towards your objectives is called for.

17 TUESDAY   *Moon Age Day 28 • Moon Sign Scorpio*

am ....

pm ....

Is your ego needing a boost? Then you have arrived at the right day because it appears that quite a few people have some good things to say about you. In some ways you fail to appreciate exactly how important you are to loved ones and friends, though it's hard to ignore the fact on this jolly day.

18 WEDNESDAY   *Moon Age Day 29 • Moon Sign Scorpio*

am ....

pm ....

Someone is trusting you to get things right today and you will not want to let them down. Not that this is likely to happen, just as long as you keep your head and remember that you are a child of Mars. It's astounding just how much you can achieve, even without going out to fight a single personal battle.

19 THURSDAY   *Moon Age Day 0 • Moon Sign Scorpio*

am ....

pm ....

If there is little to show for all your efforts at the end of today, you can at least take comfort from the fact that you are storing up glories and treasures for later. Not that you should find this to be a difficult time, just a little slower than you might wish. You do represent the ideal to someone in your vicinity!

20 FRIDAY
Moon Age Day 1 • Moon Sign Sagittarius

am . . . .

pm . . . .

Freedom from certain limitations that have been placed around you of late is the promise of today. These trends are likely to be of a distinctly personal sort and may not have any sort of bearing on your professional life, which is liable to chug along quite well. Attitude is everything concerning new projects.

21 SATURDAY ♦
Moon Age Day 2 • Moon Sign Sagittarius

am . . . .

pm . . . .

There are tests about today, even if these are not strictly of the educational sort. No matter how much others are watching your progress, you are equal to the task and should make the matter plain to everyone you come across. Remove yourself from a personal situation which you know is not to your advantage.

22 SUNDAY ♦
Moon Age Day 3 • Moon Sign Capricorn

am . . . .

pm . . . .

The Sun moves on in your personal chart and now offers a more generally expansive period, both at home and at work. This is no bad thing and sees you entering a four week period when you are able to act more like the Aries subject that you are. For today, be content with moderate gains and successes.

← NEGATIVE TREND							POSITIVE TREND →				
-5	-4	-3	-2	-1			+1	+2	+3	+4	+5
					LOVE						
					MONEY						
					LUCK						
					VITALITY						

23 MONDAY ♦ *Moon Age Day 4 • Moon Sign Capricorn*

am . . . .

pm . . . .

You are likely to find a sweeter and clearer path to your objectives than any that you have trodden for a while. Don't expect hearts and flowers in relationship terms, unless of course you are the one who is supplying them. In many ways what you get at the moment is proportional to what you give.

24 TUESDAY ♦ *Moon Age Day 5 • Moon Sign Capricorn*

am . . . .

pm . . . .

This is not a day for political discussions of any sort and you would be well advised to simply accept that others will have a different point of view from the one that you hold. Even if you do voice your opinions in truly Arian terms, you will only have to modify them when you realise the implications.

25 WEDNESDAY ♦ *Moon Age Day 6 • Moon Sign Aquarius*

am . . . .

pm . . . .

For today you are much less likely to put your foot in it. This means that you can afford to speak without having to count to ten. Realising something important about career matters, probably for the first time, encourages your mind to walk along paths and corridors that you have not explored before.

26 THURSDAY ♦ *Moon Age Day 7 • Moon Sign Aquarius*

am . . . .

pm . . . .

Look for the very best in others and that is what you are likely to find at present. You don't need to be too sensitive at the moment, since your inner mind takes care of that fact and this means that you more or less have your head to behave as you think fit. With fetters removed, it's a good time in prospect.

27 FRIDAY ♦ *Moon Age Day 8 • Moon Sign Pisces*

am . . . .

pm . . . .

Although the influence you feel you have over others is less today, you can still find ways and means to get what you want from life as a whole. Whatever you do today, over and above what is expected, it means there is less to undertake tomorrow. Keep this thought in mind and plod on regardless.

28 SATURDAY ♦ *Moon Age Day 9 • Moon Sign Pisces*

am . . . .

pm . . . .

If you tend to be rather more assertive today than you intend to be, it could be that others are forcing you to be so. The truth is that you are expected to speak your mind, and then may be criticised for doing so. If it seems as if you cannot win, you simply have to realise that life is like that sometimes.

29 SUNDAY ♦ *Moon Age Day 10 • Moon Sign Aries*

am . . . .

pm . . . .

Sunday should bring a quite and contemplative time, though this may be far from the truth now that the Moon is once again in your sign. For many of you it is a case of action from the word go. An entertaining time socially is on the cards, though some invitations will surprise you in their immediacy.

← NEGATIVE TREND							POSITIVE TREND →				
-5	-4	-3	-2	-1			+1	+2	+3	+4	+5
					LOVE						
					MONEY						
					LUCK						
					VITALITY						

30 MONDAY ♦ *Moon Age Day 11 • Moon Sign Aries*

am ....

pm ....

Very definitely in the mood to take whatever life can throw at you, there is no reason why you should balk at the possibility of standing at the front of any queue right now. You have energy, determination and the biggest smile that has been on your lips for weeks. What more could you really ask?

1 TUESDAY ♦ *Moon Age Day 12 • Moon Sign Taurus*

am ....

pm ....

In some ways it feels as though you are running out of steam, though this is only relevant for the very early part of the day. You are so busy being what you are and doing what you want, that almost everything should fall into place of its own accord. Keep a sense of proportion in relationships.

2 WEDNESDAY ♦ *Moon Age Day 13 • Moon Sign Taurus*

am ....

pm ....

A hard working sort of day, though not one that leaves you wondering where every minute went. You have the facility at present to keep track of your thoughts and emotions, so that you are fully aware of yourself at every stage. Probably a surprising time, but not at all a negative one.

3 THURSDAY ♦ *Moon Age Day 14 • Moon Sign Taurus*

am ....

pm ....

You don't have to be constantly on the go to wear yourself out. Sometimes it's a case of not stopping still long enough to realise where you are. Part of the purpose of today is to take stock. The presence of other, more contemplative types, in your life makes this process a good deal easier at present.

4 FRIDAY ♦ *Moon Age Day 15 • Moon Sign Gemini*

am ....

pm ....

Send out a message to those you love the most that you want to display your concern for them and you cannot go far wrong. The only potential difficulty that you could encounter is failing to explain yourself if you have to do something that will surprise your closest associate. You do need to talk.

5 SATURDAY ♦ *Moon Age Day 16 • Moon Sign Gemini*

am ....

pm ....

A colleague or a close friend really understands what you are trying to say at present, even on those occasions when you may not be all that certain yourself. From time to time find a place to be on your own and sit and breath deeply. This will reduce tension that has been building up inside you.

6 SUNDAY ♦ *Moon Age Day 17 • Moon Sign Cancer*

am ....

pm ....

A more reflective Arian is now on show and you really do want to understand what makes you, and others, tick. Although this is a process that does not necessarily come all that easy to you, with a little practice you can perfect the technique. An entertaining time when you find romance in the air.

← NEGATIVE TREND							POSITIVE TREND →				
-5	-4	-3	-2	-1			+1	+2	+3	+4	+5
					LOVE						
					MONEY						
					LUCK						
					VITALITY						

1998
YOUR MONTH AT A GLANCE

The twelve numbered boxes represent the important areas in your life. The key to the numbers you will find beneath the panel. A sun above the number indicates that opportunities are around. A cloud below the number, that you should be a bit defensive. Nothing above or below and life will be pretty ordinary.

☀										☀	☀
1	**2**	**3**	**4**	**5**	**6**	**7**	**8**	**9**	**10**	**11**	**12**
					☁	☁					

KEY

1 Strength of Personality
2 Personal Finance
3 Useful Information Gathering
4 Domestic Affairs
5 Pleasure & Romance
6 Effective Work & Health

7 One to One Relationships
8 Questioning, Thinking & Deciding
9 External Influences / Education
10 Career Aspirations
11 Teamwork Activities
12 Unconscious Impulses

DECEMBER HIGHS AND LOWS

Here, I show how the rhythm of the Moon will affect you this month. Like the tide, your energies and abilities will rise and fall with its pattern. When it is above the date line, go-for-it. When it is below the line you should be resting.

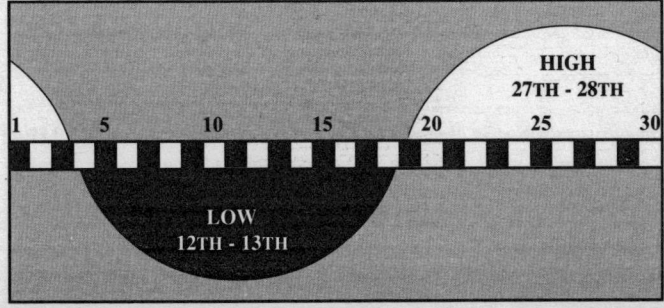

7 MONDAY ♦ *Moon Age Day 18 • Moon Sign Leo*

am ....

pm ....

There is no real reason to rush into anything today since you have all the time in the world to do things properly. What you are good at now is taking a situation that has got completely out of control and imposing a little discipline upon it. Nobody will lose out if you are careful in your methods.

8 TUESDAY ♦ *Moon Age Day 19 • Moon Sign Leo*

am ....

pm ....

Practice makes perfect, so if you are inexperienced at something you are expected to do today, simply push ahead carefully and watch yourself grow more confident by the minute. Certainly a good time to bring the light of reason to bear on an old problem and to help friends make up their minds.

9 WEDNESDAY ♦ *Moon Age Day 20 • Moon Sign Leo*

am ....

pm ....

Don't disregard the opinions of relatives or friends, or you may wish that you had listened more carefully in the fullness of time. It isn't really the considerations of others that matters, more the fact that you took the trouble to realise that your own thoughts may not always be the right ones.

10 THURSDAY ♦ *Moon Age Day 21 • Moon Sign Virgo*

am ....

pm ....

Freedom of movement is clearly very important to you now, and the needs of a busy day could get in the way of your desire for change. In a way you can structure your present wildness by deliberately putting some time aside for it. Satisfaction regarding a financial transaction is possible later in the day.

11 FRIDAY
Moon Age Day 22 • Moon Sign Virgo

am ....

pm ....

Professional details are dealt with efficiently at the end of the working week, probably leaving time in the evening when you will merely want to please yourself. By the end of the day you really want to let your hair down, which is no bad thing and probably sees the end of the day turning out memorably.

12 SATURDAY
Moon Age Day 23 • Moon Sign Libra

am ....

pm ....

The lunar low is going to help you create the ideal sort of weekend, that is if you choose to use it properly. You can't move any mountains at the moment, and it would not really be sensible to try. What you will want to have a go at is bringing a subtle but very important change to bear on yourself.

13 SUNDAY
Moon Age Day 24 • Moon Sign Libra

am ....

pm ....

Still not a dynamic time, but that does not mean that you have to sit in a chair all day and watch television. On the contrary, you are more likely to be walking along country lanes or pushing against the wind on a deserted beach. There is time to think, and moments for reflecting on present plans.

← NEGATIVE TREND						POSITIVE TREND →				
-5	-4	-3	-2	-1		+1	+2	+3	+4	+5
					LOVE					
					MONEY					
					LUCK					
					VITALITY					

14 MONDAY
Moon Age Day 25 • Moon Sign Libra

am . . . .

pm . . . .

It is in the direction of personal relationships that you turn a good deal of your attention now. The more romantic the overtures you make, the better you are going to find today to be. Single Aries subjects have the chance to look at a totally new relationship if the thought of such an eventuality appeals.

15 TUESDAY
Moon Age Day 26 • Moon Sign Scorpio

am . . . .

pm . . . .

It is hard to distinguish between social possibilities and working ones for many sons and daughters of Aries today. You find that even fairly distant colleagues can be entertaining and make very good friends. Certainly a period when it helps to keep yourself busy and during which you achieve quite a lot.

16 WEDNESDAY
Moon Age Day 27 • Moon Sign Scorpio

am . . . .

pm . . . .

Expect one or two pleasant surprises today and you won't go far wrong. Of course it is difficult to know what direction these are likely to be coming from, though it is certain that they work to your advantage. Although life itself is exciting, you remain very calm and relaxed inside yourself.

17 THURSDAY
Moon Age Day 28 • Moon Sign Sagittarius

am . . . .

pm . . . .

Your mind can be anywhere except on the job in hand, which is why some deliberate concentration is called for today. This seems terribly artificial, but will achieve the objective all the same. Keep an important matter on the boil, particularly one that relates to a decision with far reaching implications.

18 FRIDAY　　　　　*Moon Age Day 29 • Moon Sign Sagittarius*

am . . . .

pm . . . .

Not a day for getting a bee in your bonnet about anything. This would only lead to a situation from which you find it difficult to make others see your point. A little analysis of yourself will show that whatever it is you are concerned about probably isn't worth the degree of effort that you are putting in.

19 SATURDAY　　　　　*Moon Age Day 0 • Moon Sign Sagittarius*

am . . . .

pm . . . .

You probably could not begin to understand the degree of power at your disposal now when it comes to making changes in your life. Perhaps you want to dump some habit that you no longer care for, or wish to commence a new health regime. Whatever your personal goal, now is the time to go for it.

20 SUNDAY　　　　　*Moon Age Day 1 • Moon Sign Capricorn*

am . . . .

pm . . . .

Aries subjects who find themselves at work today need to be careful not to tread on the toes of superiors, some of whom might be rather too sensitive for their own, or your, good. On the other hand, if today is a time of rest, the relaxation probably turns out to be of a fairly dynamic sort.

← *NEGATIVE TREND*							*POSITIVE TREND* →			
-5	-4	-3	-2	-1		+1	+2	+3	+4	+5
					LOVE					
					MONEY					
					LUCK					
					VITALITY					

21 MONDAY   *Moon Age Day 2 • Moon Sign Capricorn*

am . . . .

pm . . . .

Someone could accuse you of being just a little too assertive at the beginning of this week, though what you are probably trying to do is to finalise plans for Christmas in a way that does not suit them. It's good to bear others in mind but there are decisions that you really will have to take all the same.

22 TUESDAY   *Moon Age Day 3 • Moon Sign Aquarius*

am . . . .

pm . . . .

This may be the start of the best period professionally that you have experienced for some time. The Sun is entering your solar tenth house and this gives you everything to play for. Friends and business associates tend to become the same thing, even if this is not the way life was previously.

23 WEDNESDAY   *Moon Age Day 4 • Moon Sign Aquarius*

am . . . .

pm . . . .

Although certain small difficulties are almost certain to surface at this time, you will not be allowing them to get in the way too much. A certain amount of anxiety can be expected and you could also expect more of yourself than it reasonable. Approach your hurdles one at a time and with sympathy for yourself.

24 THURSDAY   *Moon Age Day 5 • Moon Sign Pisces*

am . . . .

pm . . . .

Christmas Eve finds you liable to get hold of the wrong end of some stick or other. This is a minor detail and does little to hold you back as you put last minute plans into action and also manage to arrange everyone else around you. This is decisive and cheerful Aries at its very best, so keep it up.

25 FRIDAY

Moon Age Day 6 • Moon Sign Pisces

am . . . .

pm . . . .

If you had hoped to stay in the background on this Christmas Day, you are in for a surprise. The people with whom you celebrate today certainly want to make something very special of you and in your heart of hearts you probably do not mind too much. A good family day but variety appeals at some stage.

26 SATURDAY

Moon Age Day 7 • Moon Sign Pisces

am . . . .

pm . . . .

The eve of the lunar high coincides with the second day of the holiday period and puts you in the best of all positions to make your feelings known. Popularity is likely to be at an all time high and you are happy to be out there in the mainstream of life, pleasing yourself and pleasing many others too.

27 SUNDAY

Moon Age Day 8 • Moon Sign Aries

am . . . .

pm . . . .

In all probability the fact that today is a Sunday, and also falls within the Christmas period, prevents you from making the very most of all it could have offered in professional terms. You will have to use it to better personal trends instead. Ideal trends for last minute plans that mean offering a good time to all.

← NEGATIVE TREND						POSITIVE TREND →				
-5	-4	-3	-2	-1		+1	+2	+3	+4	+5
					LOVE					
					MONEY					
					LUCK					
					VITALITY					

28 MONDAY   *Moon Age Day 9 • Moon Sign Aries*

am . . . .

pm . . . .

Another great day for getting together with others, no matter what you are actually doing. Don't feel too guilty if you are still giving yourself to enjoyment because you have worked hard enough all year to justify the fact. Personal planning is possible and those around you comment on your charming approach.

29 TUESDAY   *Moon Age Day 10 • Moon Sign Taurus*

am . . . .

pm . . . .

You may have reached an important stage in your life, without having really tried to do so. It could seem as if the prospect of the New Year makes you want to sweep away old ways of thinking and instigate new ones. In fact this is a coincidence, though of course it is the effect that counts, not the reason.

30 WEDNESDAY   *Moon Age Day 11 • Moon Sign Taurus*

am . . . .

pm . . . .

A good period for putting your mind to work on short-term plans that carry you into next week. Some of you will already be back at work and noticing just how much extra responsibility is on offer. Whether you want to accept it or not really depends on the rewards that are in prospect.

31 THURSDAY   *Moon Age Day 12 • Moon Sign Gemini*

am . . . .

pm . . . .

The last day of the year and one where the advice is not to be too dogmatic about anything. There are changes in store and there is nothing that you can or would do to alter this fact. Much energy is trapped inside you at present and you can find some outlets for it this evening. Enjoy the party

RISING SIGNS
for ARIES

Look along the top to find your date of birth, and down the side fo
hour (or two) if appropriate for Summer Time.

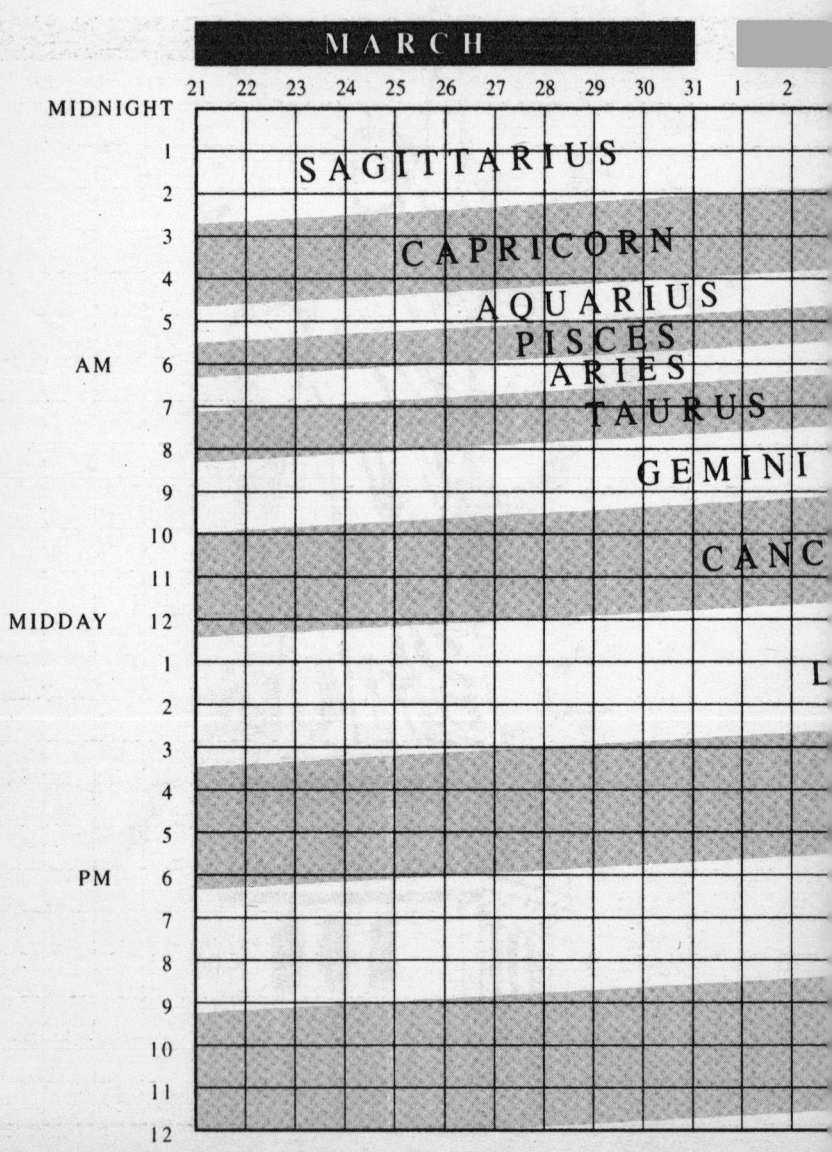

	MARCH											
	21	22	23	24	25	26	27	28	29	30	31	1	2

MIDNIGHT

1 SAGITTARIUS
2

3 CAPRICORN
4

5 AQUARIUS
   PISCES
AM 6 ARIES
7 TAURUS
8
   GEMINI
9

10
   CANC
11

MIDDAY 12

1 L
2

3

4

5

PM 6

7

8

9

10

11

12

...our GMT birth time. Where they cross is your Rising Sign. Don't forget to subtract an

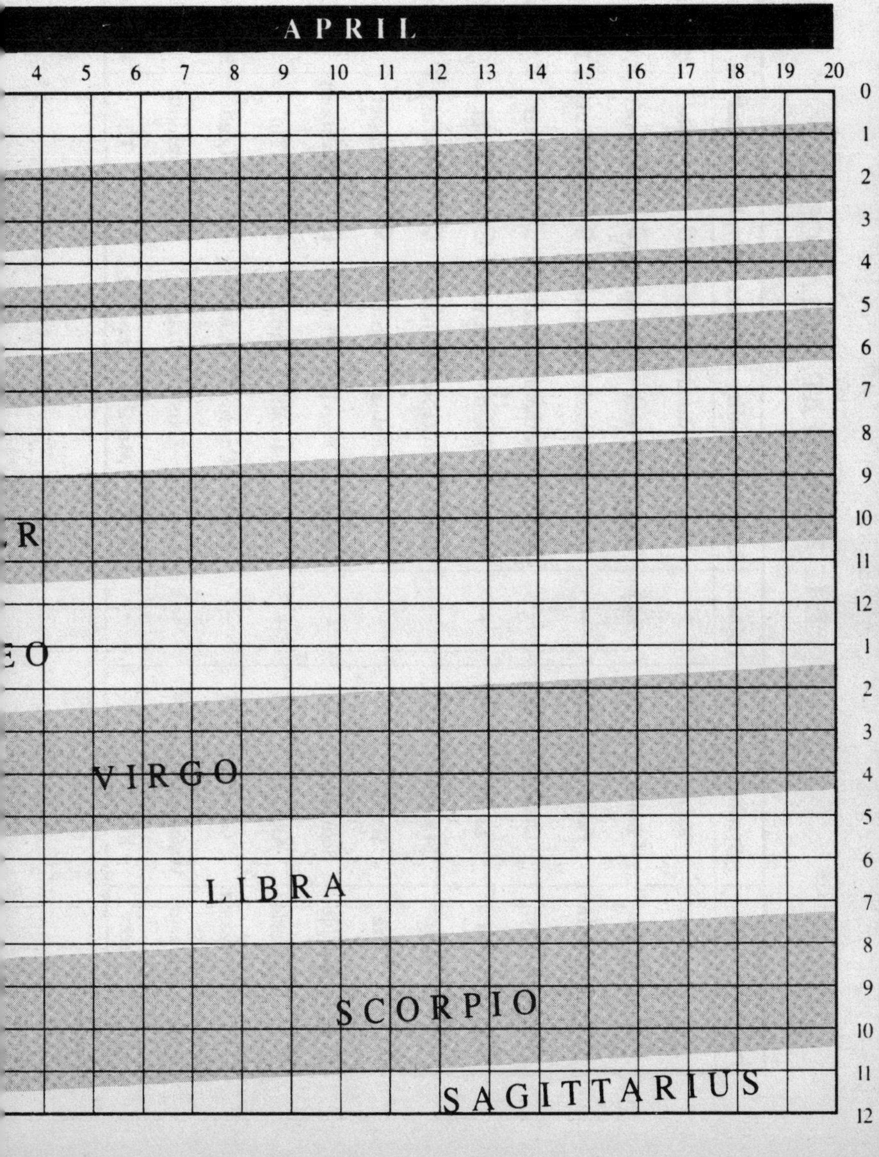

	4	5	6	7	8	9	10	11	12	13	14	15	16	17	18	19	20	

R

O

VIRGO

LIBRA

SCORPIO

SAGITTARIUS

0 1 2 3 4 5 6 7 8 9 10 11 12 1 2 3 4 5 6 7 8 9 10 11 12

THE ZODIAC AT A GLANCE

Placed	Sign	Symbol	Glyph	Polarity	Element	Quality	Planet	Glyph	Metal	Stone	Opposite
1	Aries	Ram	♈	+	Fire	Cardinal	Mars	♂	Iron	Bloodstone	Libra
2	Taurus	Bull	♉	–	Earth	Fixed	Venus	♀	Copper	Sapphire	Scorpio
3	Gemini	Twins	♊	+	Air	Mutable	Mercury	☿	Mercury	Tiger's Eye	Sagittarius
4	Cancer	Crab	♋	–	Water	Cardinal	Moon	☽	Silver	Pearl	Capricorn
5	Leo	Lion	♌	+	Fire	Fixed	Sun	☉	Gold	Ruby	Aquarius
6	Virgo	Maiden	♍	–	Earth	Mutable	Mercury	☿	Mercury	Sardonyx	Pisces
7	Libra	Scales	♎	+	Air	Cardinal	Venus	♀	Copper	Sapphire	Aries
8	Scorpio	Scorpion	♏	–	Water	Fixed	Pluto	♇	Plutonium	Jasper	Taurus
9	Sagittarius	Archer	♐	+	Fire	Mutable	Jupiter	♃	Tin	Topaz	Gemini
10	Capricorn	Goat	♑	–	Earth	Cardinal	Saturn	♄	Lead	Black Onyx	Cancer
11	Aquarius	Waterbearer	♒	+	Air	Fixed	Uranus	♅	Uranium	Amethyst	Leo
12	Pisces	Fishes	♓	–	Water	Mutable	Neptune	♆	Tin	Moonstone	Virgo

THE ZODIAC, PLANETS
AND CORRESPONDENCES

In the first column of the table of correspondence, I list the signs of the Zodiac as they order themselves around their circle; starting with Aries and finishing with Pisces. In the last column, I list the signs as they will appear as opposites to those in the first column. For example, the sign which will be positioned opposite Aries, in a circular chart will be Libra.

Each sign of the Zodiac is either positive or negative. This by no means suggests that they are either 'good' or 'bad', but that they are either extrovert, outgoing, masculine signs (positive), or introspective, receptive, feminine signs (negative).

Each sign of the Zodiac will belong to one of the four Elements: Fire, Air, Earth or Water. Fire signs are creative and enthusiastic; Air signs are mentally active and thoughtful; Earth signs are constructive and practical; Water signs are emotional and have strong feelings.

Each sign of the Zodiac also belongs to one of the Qualities: Cardinal, Fixed or Mutable. Cardinal signs are initiators and pioneers; Fixed signs are consistent and inflexible; Mutable signs are educators and live to serve.

So, each sign will be either positive or negative, and will belong to one of the Elements and to one of the Qualities. You can see from the table, for example, that Aries is a positive, Cardinal, Fire sign.
The table also shows which planets rule each sign. For example, Mars is the ruling planet of Aries. Each planet represents a particular facet of personality - Mars represents physical energy and drive - and the sign which it rules is the one with which it has most in common,

The table also shows which metals and gem stones are associated with, or correspond with the signs of the Zodiac. Again, the correspondence is made when a metal or stone possesses properties that are held in common with a particular sign of the Zodiac. This system of correspondences can be extended to encompass any group, whether animal, vegetable or mineral - as well as people! For example, each sign of the Zodiac is associated with particular flowers and herbs, with particular animals, with particular towns and countries, and so on.

It is an interesting exercise when learning about astrology, to guess which sign of the Zodiac rules a particular thing, by trying to match its qualities with the appropriate sign.

0891 229 723: *ring Old Moore now* – for the most authentic personal phone horoscope ever made available

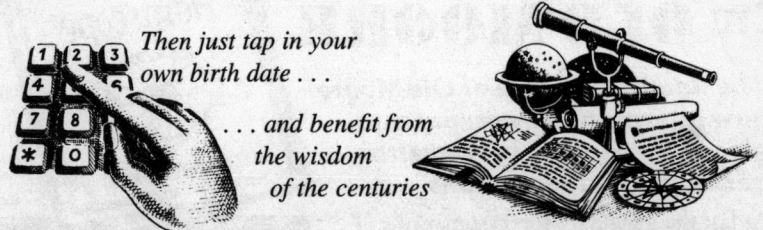

Then just tap in your own birth date . . .

. . . and benefit from the wisdom of the centuries

The uncanny foresights of Britain's N⁰1 astrologer – focused directly on your own <u>individual</u> birth-chart

Unique personalised reading

There's never been a better way to exploit your personal horoscope opportunities.

Old Moore now has a massive new computer with which he can produce a personal forecast based on the actual day of your birth. No other phone service can produce this level of accuracy. But then again, you would expect Old Moore to be ahead of the pack.

Any day of the week, Old Moore can update you on the planetary influences which surround you and point up the opportunities which will be open to you.

Unique record of prediction

The principles of astral interpretation laid down by Old Moore three centuries ago have proved amazingly reliable and accurate right up to the present day. That's how the Almanac continues to astound the world, year after year. And that's how the Old Moore system can be harnessed to the analysis of your own personal world.

Your weekly rendezvous with Old Moore

For just 36p per minute* you can hear this authoritative overview of your life, work and happiness, complete with advice on lucky dates and numbers, and the charting of your energy rhythms. Not the usual 'fortune-telling' patter. But enlightened insights into how best to exploit the future.

Remember, unlike any other phone-astrologer, Old Moore will ask you for the *day, month and year* of your birth. To give you the most individual predictions ever made possible at the lift of a phone.

So touch hands with the immortal Old Moore. Ring this number and get the benefit of a truly personalised forecast, based on the world's most acclaimed astrological tradition.

This service is only available on a touch tone button phone.

0891 229 723

*Calls cost 39p per minute cheap rate, 49p at all other times.